A Feminist Ethic
for
Social Science Research

Nebraska Sociological Feminist Collective

A Feminist Ethic
for
Social Science Research

Nebraska Sociological Feminist Collective

Women's Studies
Volume 1

The Edwin Mellen Press
Lewiston/Lampeter/Queenston

Library of Congress Cataloging-in-Publication Data

A Feminist ethic for social science research/Nebraska Sociological
    Feminist Collective.
          p.   cm -- (Women's studies ; v. 1)
    Bibliography: p.
    Includes index.
    ISBN 0-88946-120-1
    1. Feminism--Philosophy. 2. Feminism--Research. 3. Women's
studies. 4. Social science research. I. Nebraska Sociological
Feminist Collective. II. Series: Women's studies (Lewiston, N.Y.) ;
v. 1.
HQ1154.F4456 1988
305.4'2'01--dc 19

                                                            87-27377
                                                                 CIP

This is volume 1 in the continuing series
Women's Studies
Volume 1 ISBN 0-88946-120-1
WS Series ISBN 0-88946-118-X

© Copyright 1988 The Edwin Mellen Press.

All Rights Reserved. For more information contact

    The Edwin Mellen Press   The Edwin Mellen Press
        Box 450   Box 67
      Lewiston, NY   Queenston, Ontario
      USA 14092   CANADA L0S 1L0

            The Edwin Mellen Press, Ltd.
             Lampeter, Dyfed, Wales,
            UNITED KINGDOM SA48 7DY

        Printed in the United States of America

A Feminist Ethic
for
Social Science Research

Nebraska Sociological Feminist Collective

Table of Contents

Preface   ix

Empowering a Feminist Ethic for Social Science Research:
Nebraska Sociological Feminist Collective
by Beth Hartung, Jane C. Ollenburger, Helen A. Moore
and Mary Jo Deegan   1

Part One: The Objectification of Wimmin

The Deep Structure of Gender Antithesis:
Another View of Capitalism and Patriarchy
by Dorothy E. Smith   23

Researching Prostitution:
Some Problems for Feminist Research
by Carol Smart   37

Lesbian Research Ethics
by Pauline Bart   47

On the Ethics of Research on the
Triple Oppression of Black American Women
by Linda Williams   54

Part Two: Research By, For and About Wimmin

A Feminist Research Ethos
by Ann R. Bristow and Jody A. Esper   67

Research as Critical Reflection:
A Study of Self, Time and Communicative Competency
by Valerie Ann Malhotra   82

Consideration of Ethical Issues in the Assessment
of Feminist Projects: A Case Study Using Illuminative Evaluation
by Joan Poliner Shapiro and Beth Reed   100

Part Three: Feminism, Language and Ideas

Prescribed Passivity: The Language of Sexism
by Julia Penelope — 119

Gender Bias as a Threat to Construct Validity in Research Design
by Judith A. Levy — 139

Sociology of Medicine for Whom?:
Feminist Perspectives in a Multi-Paradigmatic Sociology of Medicine
by Juanne N. Clarke — 158

Lesbianism, Feminism and Social Science
by Vera Whisman — 174

Part Four: Gatekeeping in Employment, Publication and Research

Feminism and Sociology:
An Unfortunate Case of Nonreciprocity
by Mary White Stewart — 187

Am I My Sister's Gatekeeper?:
Cautionary Tales from the Academic Hierarchy
by Judith A. Cook and Mary Margaret Fonow — 201

Bibliography — 219

Contributors' Notes — 237

Index — 245

Preface

We preface this volume with a note on our herstory, an explanation of our use of feminist spelling ("wimmin/womon"), and our heartfelt thanks to persons participating in this effort. The book you now hold represents several years of work for a number of people. We hope that it aids and augments feminist, activist research.

Our Story

The current Nebraska Sociological Feminist Collective formed in the spring of 1982. Our initial purpose was to write an article articulating some of our anger at the misuse and abuse of wimmin within sociology[1]. Since that time, a number of changes have occurred, not the least of which has been the trial of working as a collective separated by hundreds of miles. The following is a brief history of our collective process (not the collective process), and in particular, what happens to working collectively when members are geographically mobile. At this writing, we are not a true collective. In working on this manuscript, we have developed a division of labor as democratically as possible and we write and speak to each other often, but we miss the group dynamic that facilitates collective work at its best.

In 1982 we were five. Each of us brought very different resources to the collective, but we shared a commitment to feminism, to sociology, and to our first act as a group: to write. Two of our members, Mary Jo and Jane, had worked together in a previous collective. In the spring of 1982 Mary Jo was a tenured associate professor, and Jane was an advanced doctoral student. Helen was an assistant professor, not yet tenured; Beth, a first year doctoral student. Cynthia Trainor, the fifth collective member, was an M.A. student. We met many times through the spring and summer of 1982, faced with the trying task of synthesizing five different writing styles. As we drafted and worked through our article we discussed the need to articulate a _feminist_ research ethic for the social sciences in opposition to the standing androcentric one. Very early in our collective, then, we were committed to a task that would involve two years of work -- editing a special issue of a journal.

Mary Jo had edited special issues of journals in the past, and we relied on her expertise in putting a proposal together. At the time, we also discussed our respective abilities to commit to such a long term goal. Cynthia withdrew to pursue activist work outside the university. We wished her well. And we were four.

Humanity and Society, the journal of humanist sociologists, accepted our proposal for a special issue on Feminist Research Ethics after we had demonstrated to the editorial board's satisfaction that a feminist ethic was indeed different from a humanist ethic. The real work of the collective began. From the fall of 1982 until the spring of 1984, each of us assumed responsibility for voluminous amounts of correspondence, publicizing the special issue, contacting reviewers, working with manuscripts, and typesetting. Through the spring of 1983 we were able to do this face to face and as a group. Problems that arose were discussed by all of us, including problems of differential resources.

Collective work in the context of our hierarchically structured institution makes different resources and differential allocation of work inevitable. Thus, power issues have been salient in the collective to varying degrees and at different times. Being cognizant of the issues helped avoid problems with them. Mary Jo and Helen, as faculty members, had a greater range of contacts for soliciting reviewers and invited manuscripts. Jane and Beth, graduate students when the process began, had limited contacts in the discipline and could not apply for institutional support. Initially, each of us contributed only the strengths we had, although through the collective process, each of us developed new strengths as we worked together. Working as a collective was not always without discord, however; and it became more difficult to make group decisions when members of the collective were absent.

In the fall of 1982, having completed her Ph.D., Jane took a post-doctoral fellowship at Iowa State. Through 1982-83, she commuted between Ames and Lincoln so that the collective was able to continue meeting sporadically as a group. In the fall of 1983, however, Jane left the region to take a position as an assistant professor. Her physical absence was the first step in changing the collective. In addition, Mary Jo was away from Nebraska during the summers, and was awarded a sabbatical leave in 1984. This left Helen and Beth at the University of Nebraska, our "home" address.

In the spring of 1983, Mary Jo, Helen and Beth completed the compilation of the special issue of Humanity and Society and sent it to the editors camera ready. Jane had contributed a great deal of work from her end in the form of writing and correspondence. Here we could have stopped our group work. We had agreed to work together to edit the special issue, and beyond that, we chose not to take on new research tasks. Nonetheless, we decided even with the distance to continue our efforts to publish a substantially edited version of the journal as a book. All of us believed in the manuscript, and many of our contributors had been asked to substantially cut their articles to fit the journal format. A book would enable considerable expansion and revision of their work.

By the fall of 1984, the time commitment required of the collective was minimal. We no longer needed to meet weekly, and indeed we could not. Each of us took responsibility for locating potential publishers and writing to contributors. Together we worked on the book proposal, but the majority of our active work as a collective was behind us.

Through the academic year 1984-85, the collective met infrequently as we heard from publishers or contributors. Each of us had other concerns impinging on our lives, and the publishing process involved long periods when we heard from no one. That year, Helen was preparing her tenure dossier, Beth finished her Ph.D. and left Nebraska for a position in Illinois, Jane was still in North Carolina, and Mary Jo was in Minnesota working on <u>Women and Symbolic Interaction</u> (1987). Our lives, and the tasks of the collective became increasingly fragmented of necessity. Helen inherited the task of coordinating our efforts as we sent copies of correspondence back and forth in quadruplicate. It was sometimes difficult to remember who had agreed to do what, and in what time frame. We have yet to sort out what recent changes in the collective mean to us as a group (Beth has moved on to Fresno, California, and Jane has returned to her home state of Minnesota), but we are glad we have persevered. It has not always been easy, but it has almost always been rewarding.

Communicating by letter and by phone does not replace the intimacy of seeing each other, of gathering together in one place. Interaction becomes more complex when indirect, and the likelihood of communication breaking down does increase. With that said, we have managed to retain a connectedness despite distance, and that connectedness comes through a shared history and our commitment to feminist scholarship. When our efforts began five years ago, we believed in the equitable pooling of ideas and work. We believed that the product of our labor, shaped by reviewers, contributors and other colleagues, would be something more than any of us could have done as individuals. This manuscript is testament to that belief. Now that this project is complete, the Nebraska Feminist Sociological Collective disbands for the moment. Our dispersal does not mean that the four of us will not continue to work together, nor does it mean the Nebraska Feminist Sociological Collective will not continue with new participants as new feminists enter the discipline.

Given the geographic distance between co-editors of this volume, we will not be able to continue as one collective. An agreed upon division of labor does not a collective make.

Instead, we will draw upon resources we have nearby —our feminist colleagues in our geographic community. The collective process empowers because it is an outward and upward spiral. Each of us as individuals gained knowledge and strength from working with the other three. Each of us will do this again, using the skills and patience learned in the Nebraska Collective. At this writing, we last met as a group in the spring of 1986. We agreed at that meeting to continue our efforts to publish this manuscript but beyond that, not to start any new projects together. The mood was one of some sadness mixed with relief and elation. And these feelings sum up what is good and positive in the collective experience.

Womon/Wimmin

We have chosen in our writings to use the alternative spellings of womon (traditionally woman) and wimmin (traditionally women). These spellings are phonetic and are pronounced in the traditional fashion. At first, their appearance is disconcerting if not shocking and often cause editors and reviewers to reach for their blue pencils. However, we have reasons for our alternative spellings. First, there are no m-e-n in our wimmin and there is no m-a-n in our womon. We find the words "wo-men" and "wo-man" to reflect again the impression that one can do little given the English language without including men. Second, the Revised Edition of the Random House

College Dictionary informs us that one of the origins of the word "woman" is the Old English wifman which equals "wif female + man human being"[2]. The dictionary then refers us to the words "wife" and "man". It stands to reason that in feminist discourse we have come too far to be referred to as the "wife of man" and that these origins are again a reflection of the sexist nature of the language.

Our critics attempt to trivialize these changes by embracing the mythical "generics" such as "man," "mankind" and "he". We respond, as Sheila Rowbotham claims, that "Language conveys a certain power" (Rowbotham, 1973: 32). Clearly the issue of alternative spellings for womon/wimmin as well as the issue of the mythical generics are political issues. The arguments regarding the gendering of language date back to ancient Greek philosophers. "Aristotle, for example, regarded the ending of a word as a criterion of classification. He contrasted 'the male, as it moves and acts' to the 'female, as it suffers' (Janssen-Jurreit, 1982: 290)." Julia Penelope (Stanley) in her chapter, "Prescribed Passivity," reprinted in this volume, gives us a contemporary denunciation of the masculine generic and clearly places the issue in the realm of the political. Throughout the history of Western political thought we find wimmin's language/world trivialized (Elshtain, 1982). From this, it should not be surprising that (a) we claim the English language to be sexist, and (b) this sexism is related to the ethics of research in the social sciences, and (c) we will change, mold and manipulate language in order to influence its evolution and its effects. "Meanings evolve slowly as changing social practices, relations, and institutions are characterized in new ways. Over time this helps to give rise to an altered reality, for language evolution is central to reality (Elshtain, 1982: 616)."

We summarize the above arguments in the words of Judith McDaniel in her presentation to the 1977 Modern Language Association Convention session on Lesbians and Literature: "If feminism is the final cause--and I believe it is--then language is the first necessity (McDaniel, 1978: 17)."

NOTES

[1] Nebraska Sociological Feminist Collective. 1983. "A feminist ethic for social science research," *International Women's Studies Quarterly*, 14: 57-72.

[2] The Random House College Dictionary Revised Edition (1975). Jess Stein, Editor-in-Chief: p. 1514.

Empowering a Feminist Ethic For Social Science Research: Nebraska Sociological Feminist Collective

Beth Hartung, Jane C. Ollenburger, Helen A. Moore and Mary Jo Deegan.

An ethic defines the general nature of the morals, rules and standards governing the conduct and choices of individuals as well as members of a profession (Oxford English Dictionary, 1971). A feminist ethic for social science research specifically orders these general issues to recognize and account for wimmin's continued oppression within a patriarchal social system and academic disciplines. A feminist ethic identifies this continued oppression as a major contradiction of our research, work and social structure. Within social sciences generally, and sociology specifically, little attention is paid to the underlying patriarchal ethic which informs theory, method and substantive issues.

We preface this collection with a definition of the assumptions that underlie a feminist ethic for research and study. Our discussion amplifies four key issues: (1) the objectification of wimmin as research objects; (2) research by, for, and about wimmin; (3) language as used and abused in sociology; and (4) the gatekeeping process in employment, funding and research. In reality, these areas are inseparable. This book reflects the overlap among them, enhancing its continuity and comprehensiveness.

* Some portions of this paper are derived from "A feminist ethic for social science research," Women's Studies International Forum. Vol. 6 (1983): 535-543.

Feminist scholarship is at cross-purposes with traditional social science. This observation is neither surprising nor profound, but it is the basis for a complex set of problems which need continual re-analysis in the social sciences. The authors in this book are mostly academic sociologists and psychologists who examine their disciplines to illustrate historically-situated problems of patriarchal bias and plausible ethical responses. An ethical agenda is introduced here and elaborated throughout the readings which follow. Each author/researcher also provides a reflexive statement of political and ideological commitment to her topic.

In this introductory essay, we focus on sociology, our own discipline, to frame and introduce the articles which follow. Sociology is particularly culpable, having made public claims to address the problems of minorities and oppressed people. During the past two decades, sociologists have generated significant discussions of the politics and ethics of doing research on sex, class and race (Rainwater and Yancey, 1967; Gornick and Moran, 1971; Ladner, 1973; Acker, 1973; Millman and Kanter, 1975). However, the recent publication of the revised Code of Ethics of the American Sociological Association (ASA footnotes, April, 1982) does not reflect the power or the substance of these arguments. This revised code was an effort "to sensitize all sociologists to the ethical issues that may arise in their work" and to examine those principles which "may occasionally conflict with more general ethical concerns."

For those feminist scholars trained in the social scientific framework, which is historically bounded by a patriarchal academy, the conflicts presented by the ASA agenda are personal and political, public and private. An academic feminist is indeed a contradiction (Freeman, 1979; Leffler et al., 1973). Academia is fed by the scientific status quo with occasional pretensions to the safety of liberalism, e.g., revised ethical codes. In contrast, feminism is fundamentally subversive and critical. As scholars we are marginal insiders at best, speaking the language of our particular discipline. As wimmin we are outsiders, marked by "otherness" (Westkott, 1979). "From the start, persons who are sorted into the male class and persons who are sorted into the other are given different treatment, acquire different experience, enjoy and suffer different expectations" (Goffman, 1977:303; emphasis added). As feminists, we are compelled to take a critical, activist stance which both encompasses and transcends sociology.

In the following discussion, we explicitly attack the traditional canons of sociology. Our cultural background in the United States and the cultural bias of the sociological discipline threaten to narrow our focus. But the goal and framework of the feminist ethic are by no means restricted to sociology or sociology as practiced in the United States. Sociology is only one vehicle for implementing a feminist ethic which crosses discipline boundaries and draws upon the experiences of wimmin throughout first, second and third world nations.

Our discussion revolves around the pursuit and use of knowledge. We propose a feminist ethic that restores the balance between the means and ends of research, confronts the racist, imperialist, classist, able-bodist, heterosexist and sexist assumptions prevalent in the social science research agenda (revised or not) and combats patriarchal and masculinist structures inside and outside the academy. Rejecting "business as usual" in the study of wimmin means that data collection for the sake of knowledge alone cannot be tolerated. The research act must be a social, economic, and political act which, as a priority, empowers wimmin outside of the academy.

THE OBJECTIFICATION OF WIMMIN

The revised ASA code exhorts sociologists to "strive to maintain objectivity and integrity" and to adhere to "the highest possible technical standards in research." The *a priori* status of quantitative and technical methods at the apex of sociological ethics generates a hierarchy of acceptance and circulation of positivist methods and assumptions. Social science researchers use the rhetoric of objectivity to legitimate their vested interests and contributions to knowledge. A feminist analysis and ethic must demystify objectivity in sociology, which can mask the objectification of wimmin and all minorities.

The definition, use and rationalization of objectivity dichotomizes the researcher's view of the world. For example, in sociology (Smith, 1974a; Reinharz, 1985), history (Lerner, 1979), anthropology (Slocum, 1980), linguistics (Penelope, 1978), and other social sciences (Spender, 1981b; Lowe and Hubbard, 1983), women as research object represents either a deviation from the male standard (norm), or she is subsumed by the male-biased research paradigm. The gap between knower and known becomes ever more rigid in the pursuit of objectivity; the scientist becomes expert in knowing wimmin's lives. Wimmin (as researchers and as subjects) are implicitly removed from active roles in the traditionally male spheres of analysis and technical research.

As research subjects, research assistants, or as helpful (and often unnamed) spouses in dissertation and manuscript acknowledgements, wimmin's contributions are manipulated or made invisible. The male is socially recognized as the rational manipulator of data and the source of legitimate resources, skills and funding (Goldsmith, 1980). This research bias excludes wimmin from revising oppressive and distorting methodologies.

The lack of research by and about the "other" (wimmin, minorities, the working class, the disabled, lesbians and gays) until the last two decades leaves us relatively bereft of information for these groups. In many subdisciplines of sociology we lack baseline data (e.g., Daniels, 1975; Roberts, 1981 a, b) yet the rich oral and folk information in wimmin's lives are discredited as data bases. Whether these omissions are "more puerile than prejudicial, more accidental than intentional" is unresolved (McCormack, 1975). Feminist researchers must remove the "people = male" bias and acknowledge wimmin's voices (Silvira, 1980) to highlight the class, race and other significant differences among our lives.

The diverse range of issues in feminist research ethics is reflected in the first set of readings in this volume. Smith persuasively argues in her work "The deep structure of gender antitheses" that capitalism and patriarchy form one side of a dialectic in opposition to feminism. Feminist antitheses require a new way of speaking in the social sciences. In her essay on prostitution entitled "Researching prostitution: Some problems for feminist research," Smart focuses on the contradictions of long and short-term goals of feminist research activities. While acknowledging the personal distress of hearing the voices of those who "enforce the law," she works to identify the current legal, social and economic conditions of prostitutes. She then raises the long-term agenda of confronting women's bodies as commodities. She calls for a flexible system of feminist ethics, including the study of powerful men and the institutions they control.

Bart, in her article "Lesbian research ethics," proposes that feminist research stands to demystify the world _for_ wimmin, and that being a lesbian researcher requires more than being a "good" researcher. She focuses on key issues of responsibility to research subjects and research training within the academic enterprise. Williams provides a classic statement on the importance of Black wimmin within the social sciences in her essay "On the ethics of research on the triple oppression of Black American women." The range of family and work roles held by Black wimmin have been distorted by Anglo-centric and androcentric public policy research. A focus on theory and praxis within the capitalist, racist and sexist economy forms the focus of her critique.

RESEARCH BY, FOR AND ABOUT WIMMIN

The issue of power is integral to research and is a key to confronting the various oppressions inherent in that agenda. Through the patriarchal research process, the responsibility for defining, accusing, disciplining and eradicating anti-womon activities is left to the powerless. Research subjects, research assistants and "others" do not participate in the human subjects review processes within institutions, nor in the grant review activities of major funding agencies. Their critique of the ethics or process of a research project is unheard, enabling the researcher and the research institution to maintain a patriarchal enterprise (Reinharz, 1985).

Critiquing sociology as practiced begs the question of how we can empower a feminist ethic. To what extent are wimmin exploited on the grounds of enlightened academic self-interest? To what extent does research on wimmin through the auspices of traditional institutions benefit wimmin? These are questions of ethical conduct.

The revised ASA code remains ambiguous about harassment and exploitation, despite specific discussions of norms and behaviors regarding sexual abuse and its economic consequences for victims (Evans, 1978). This exploitation must be tied explicitly to the oppressions of sex, race, class, sexual preference and rank. The ASA code defaults responsibility for these definitions, accusations and redress to the powerless. A feminist ethic acknowledges these oppressions by analyzing and breaking down the age, sex and rank groupings within the academy. This is particularly true for graduate students and non-tenured faculty whose work is often misappropriated or maligned as non-academic. In addition, the contributions of "others" in the office, in the field, and as informants must be validated, fairly compensated and publicly acknowledged.

According to the ASA code, we "must not make any guarantees to subjects. . . unless there is full intention and ability to honor such commitments." In a feminist ethic, we must not undertake research until and unless we can make guarantees to our informants. In the past, advocacy research has been relegated to the sidelines as "non-academic" and the ties between theory and praxis have been denied. Feminist scholars often lose professional legitimation for their research when they return investments to wimmin and contribute to significant social change.

The research of male academicians/technicians on wimmin is often an invasion of wimmin's privacy. The sexual objectification of wimmin in the behavioral sciences is a clear example of the outcome of cross-sex research in which a feminist ethic is not employed. We encourage wimmin in the social sciences to recognize their own "insider" roles, talents and perceptions and to engage in a research dialogue that empowers all wimmin. We must acknowledge the advantages and responsibilities of our participation in sexual, familial, academic and political relations which inform our ideas.

In the second set of readings, we are provided both specific and general maps for feminist ethics in the research process. When examining the interaction of violence and sexism in rape, Bristow and Esper approach the research process with a heightened consciousness of oppression in "A feminist research ethos." They contrast the "interrogation" of "respondents" with a true dialogue that regards research participants as experts on their own experiences. These dialogues are extended to the internal dialogue of the researcher (critical awareness) and dialogues with society (reporting). In her article "Research as critical reflection: A Study of time, self and communicative competency," Malhotra integrates symbolic interaction, phenomenology, and critical theory to define research as a critically reflective process. By incorporating participants in each stage of the research process, the line between "researcher" and "participant" was continually erased. By reviewing and using multi-methodological approaches to alleviate repressive and exploitive aspects of research about oppressed groups, the small groups empowered themselves in their everyday lives. Shapiro and Reed turn their attention to the practice of evaluating feminist activities in "Illuminative evaluation: Meeting the special needs of feminist projects." In their model, they combine qualitative and quantitative techniques and discuss the stance of the objective feminist evaluator in her roles as critic, colleague and consultant. Their analysis includes the role of staff input to the research process and its benefits.

FEMINISM, LANGUAGE AND IDEAS

Language is a critical dimension wherein the patriarchal values and prejudices embodied in the discipline come to light. Offensive language goes hand-in-hand with oppresive research and theory. Sociological language reflects the patriarchal features of language in general, as well as creating its own unique ethical problems. The generic use of "man," "mankind," and "he" as well as the spelling of "woman" and "women" illustrate the historical trend of men to aggrandize their own sex (Penelope, 1978). Even when sociological research demonstrates the effects of language on consciousness, these efforts are ignored or labeled "trivial". Schneider and Hacker (1973) tested the hypothesis that "generic" man is generally understood to include wimmin, but found that the concept "man" clearly meant male individuals.

Sociologists consistently use the passive voice in writing and reporting research and theory. The researcher removes the self from the report, creating an illusion of objectivity. Thus it appears that "institutions act" instead of sociologists interpreting actions conducted in, and enforced by, institutions. The researcher can abdicate responsibility for the ethical and political concerns of research subjects. The passive voice also invokes the ambigious "they" or the unnamed "expert."

Thus, in sociology and other academic disciplines, wimmin are symbolically annihilated, i.e., (1) under-represented or absent; (2) trivialized and victimized; or (3) delegated to "hearth and home" (Tuchman, Daniels and Benet, 1978; Stimpson, 1980). Through the narrow selection of sociological questions, wimmin are omitted from the research agenda or confined to the areas of family or sex role development. Wimmin's position in social stratification, productive home labor, racial and ethnic groups, etc., has historically been subsumed under their family status (i.e., the husband's status).

The use of oppressive language and ideas has important implications for the theoretical development of sociology as well as for the public policies which are derived from sociological research. By defining norms and values for wimmin through the authority granted to objective science, sociology supports the oppression of wimmin. By inhibiting the understanding of our oppression(s), this oppression is especially severe for wimmin who are multiply oppressed (Deegan, 1985).

Wimmin of color are consistently misrepresented by sociologists. For example, the 1965 Moynihan report explained Black economic problems as a consequence of a pathological family structure with absent fathers and domineering mothers (Moynihan, 1965; 1968). By virtue of a "strong matriarchal drive", Black wimmin were accused by white sociologists of "castrating" Black men (Rainwater and Yancey, 1967). Wallace (1978) and Hooks (1981) critique the sociological myth of the Black womon as "castrator" and "matriarch" both for its normative distortions and its significant negative effect on the Black political movement in the United States. Wallace also notes that white male researchers have appealed to Black men's sense of patriarchy, thereby forcing Black wimmin to rank their oppressions.

Lesbians are also oppressed by the language and theory of sociology and are subsumed under the topic of (male) homosexuality in the area of deviance. Lesbians and gays are classified as deviants from the heterosexual norm and contact with them leads to a "contagion of stigma" (Kirby and Corzine, 1981). The sociological language used to study homosexuality implicitly takes the homophobic, heterosexist and masculinist perspective, omitting lesbians from discussions of family, reproduction and politics. By focusing on the research subject as "other" and by using the "people = male" paradigm, the sociologist perpetuates his/her ethical distance and can ignore the lived consequences of research for wimmin and minorities.

Sociology as a discipline perpetuates an elitist concern for positivist science, rather than tendering revolutionary or socially responsible analysis. In "Prescribed passivity: The language of sexism" Julia Penelope (Stanley) argues that "generics" such as "man" and "mankind" document the structure of thought giving power to men. The use of these words in advertisements, literature, and formal theory augment the spoken word. The female is the antithesis of the male in our language, so what is defined as male is defined positively. Language shapes a disturbingly negative reality for those who are female, reflecting an entrenched patriarchal "semantic space." Levy then further delineates the gender bias common to domain assumptions, language structures and operationalization in her article entitled "Gender bias as a threat to construct validity in research design." While reviewing this work, she concludes that the reformulation of mainstream research must avoid the pitfalls of disadvantaging males or introducing "estrocentric" bias. The social construct of science is a political process that employs reductionist models taken from the biological and natural sciences to legitimate male power.

In the next essay, "Sociology of medicine for whom? Feminist perspectives in a multi-paradigmatic sociology of medicine," Clarke identifies the complex practice within the sociology of medicine that reflects three major sets of ideas: positivism, naturalism and activism. Each perspective has particular advantages and disadvantages, but the positivist approach is the most legitimated, financed and enacted. It is also least able to explain change or women's experiences. Critics of positivism, as well as patriarchy, find themselves in a particularly vulnerable position in terms of the ability to practice and implement their ideas. In her article "Lesbianism, feminism and social science," Whisman uses political lesbianism and anti-pornography feminism to demonstrate some parallel problems in general social theory. She concludes that these problems are often rooted in the class background of feminist theorists who may be trained in sociology. The competition over definitions by feminists, lesbians or sociologists illustrates "what happens when social theories become ideologies."

GATEKEEPING IN EMPLOYMENT, PUBLICATION AND RESEARCH

The effects of "objectivity" and lack of access for the powerless are further compounded in publication and research funding. People who certify others are gatekeepers; they control access to resources. In academia, the most important resources are jobs, publications and money. Career advancement is marked by the successful completion of stages guarded by gatekeepers who distribute these scarce resources (Caplow and McGee, 1958; Van den Berghe, 1970). To implement a feminist ethic, feminists need to successfully bypass gatekeepers, to break down barriers, and, most importantly, conceive of alternatives to the present oppressive system of power brokerage.

A sociologist's entry into the job market is linked directly to graduate training and sponsorship. A prestige system undergirds the entire gatekeeping process; institutions are ranked according to their value and achievement of excellence by positivist standards. Access to mentors and institutions (assistantships, fellowships, grants, etc.) is a key mechanism in gatekeeping. By omitting wimmin from professional full-time positions in major graduate institutions, feminist mentors are rare (Hughes, 1975; Rossi and Calderwood, 1973). Patriarchal sponsorship is called, appropriately, the "old boy" network. Thus a massive, systemic hierarchy exists prior to any student's entry into the system, and certain ideas and ways of doing sociology are defined a priori as less acceptable than others.

That effectiveness of gatekeeping can be gauged by the job placement of wimmin scholars. Wimmin graduates from elite institutions in sociology experience greater downward mobility on the job market than their male peers (Welch and Lewis, 1980). Part-time and temporary positions in sociology, as elsewhere, are "women's issues" because wimmin are over-represented in these positions (Tuchman and Tuchman, 1982). The temporary or part-time scholar is confined to piece-work teaching, which restricts research and job security. With heavier teaching loads and less institutional support for travel, research, and other professional needs, productivity in terms of written publication is difficult. Hierarchical control is maintained further in a self-perpetuating system that restricts symbols and resources of prestige. Those outside the system remain outside, those inside tend to remain inside if they adhere to narrowly defined academic norms.

Feminism is a key way of thinking about research that is suppressed within this structure, and continually held outside of it. Freeman succinctly summarizes the barriers that confront wimmin who achieve academically:

> Research on women, for example, is rarely read by male colleagues, and is largely considered to be at worse faddish, and at best narrow. Even if one has written twenty papers on extremely diverse aspects of woman's existence, it is still considered to be in the same subfield and hardly comparable to five good papers on voting statistics or Melville's novels (Freeman, 1979:29).

Students and/or faculty who question the ideological patriarchal structures are seen as "not very bright" or "not sociologists" because they do not appear to understand how a "value free" profession operates. Academics view criticisms of the system as signs of weakness in the "other" student/faculty, rather than legitimate critiques.

Journal policies operate with similar rhetoric about supposedly apolitical, objective standards of excellence. A major mechanism to ensure this egalitarian claim is the democratic peer review. Referees are selected from among recognized leaders in the field, interested readers or recommended names that gain the attention and approval of editors and their review boards. Feminist referees are rarely included since those who dominate both numerically and ideologically are not feminists, and are often bitterly anti-feminist. A circular process operates: feminist writers cannot get published, so they do not become recognized reviewers. Feminism is defined as ideological (as opposed to scientific and objective), thus feminist authors are not "excellent." The democratic review by positivist peers virtually guarantees that feminist writings are not published. Acceptance and rejection are seen to reside in the canons of knowledge and the judgment of one's peers, not as a reflection of discriminatory treatment. (We lapse into the passive voice to deliberately invoke the authority of the discipline.) This review process is, after all, the same evaluation process that others undergo. Some researchers are viewed as successful and feminists are not. Dissenting voices are stilled.

Similarly, the basic reason that feminists cannot obtain research money is that the feminist agenda conflicts with the patriarchal system. Computers, interviewers, assistants, and other research resources are outside the pocketbook range of all social scientists, but feminists bear the brunt of this discrimination. Wimmin's conflicts are evidenced in a widening range of government funding policies. Kutza thoroughly documents the gender-biased payment structure of U. S. government benefits for disabled wimmin:

Marginal improvements in program specifics will not
solve what is a continuing problem for women - the
strong relationship between program benefit
entitlement and labor force participation. As long
as the major (and most generous) disability
protection programs are premised upon a model of
life-long, full-time employment outside the home,
with disability being explicitly defined in a
work-related context, women will continue to be
disadvantaged" (Kutza, 1981: 315).

The government will not pay researchers to tell it to
spend more money on wimmin or, if needed, less on men.

Research support often comes from feminist action
programs and we must enlarge these efforts. Wimmin's
inequalities will otherwise be systematically and
deliberately ignored or reinforced by mainstream academic
research. In a capitalist society, public and private
funds are denied to researchers who empower wimmin. In
the final set of papers, Stewart argues in "Feminism and
Sociology: An unfortunate case of non-reciprocity" that
feminist efforts within sociology have been suppressed,
yet the possibility remains for compatible and mututally
reinforcing work. Feminists have vigorously participated
in creative sociological research, often crossing
disciplinary lines to enlarge their analyses. In
contrast, many sociologists have maintained a defensive
posture and created barriers to the incorporation of
feminist conclusions. In their article entitled "Am I my
sister's gatekeeper? Cautionary tales from the academic
hierarchy," Cook and Fonow argue that to safeguard
feminist discourse, we must stimulate and protect its

production by critically analyzing the process of feminist scholarship. While highlighting the structure of patriarchal authority and scientism, they also caution against the arbitrary and unpredictable nature of gatekeeping.

CONCLUSIONS

A feminist ethic differs from the traditional sociological ethic in several fundamental ways. Traditional social scientists seek knowledge for the advancement and enlightenment of the discipline itself; in contrast, feminists analyze social oppression to empower wimmin and minorities. The traditional scientist is accountable only to the profession. The feminist sociologist is also accountable to her peers, the wimmin's movement, a feminist ethic, wimmin, and oppressed peoples.

In this introduction, we framed key biases and assumptions prevalent in sociology as practiced in the United States. Established ethics continue to uphold objectivity as the pinnacle of sociological research. To this end, an artificial dichotomy between theory and practice is maintained. Wimmin's work as secretaries, interviewers, wives, and graduate students is defined as unimportant and thus exploitable by researchers. The research conclusions generated by studies of wimmin continue to reflect male resources, biases and lack of reflexiveness. Likewise, sociological language omits wimmin, trivializes their oppression, defines them primarily in relation to a husband and family, and perpetuates harmful myths about wimmin. Finally, through the gatekeeping process, feminist work is kept out of publication and widespread circulation. The result is that the patriarchal sociological method continues unchallenged for the most part.

There are several levels on which feminists can and do put a feminist ethic into practice. Despite existing barriers, feminist sociologists can walk a thin line between co-optation and expulsion from the field. Many feminists are politically active outside the discipline, working for long-term changes. Others work behind the scenes. Practicing feminist ethics inside the academy will not provide prestige or advancement in the field. We make myriad small compromises to gain and hold positions in sociology. Our danger lies in our privileged positions; we must analyze and challenge the underlying patriarchal structure of those positions. Our challenge lies in working for significant change inside and outside the academy even as we are a part of it.

EMPOWERING A FEMINIST ETHIC

The following are suggestions/challenges to all who labor in the discipline:

End the Objectification/Exploitation of Wimmin in Research:

Learn, accept and use qualitative, historical and other methodologies which highlight wimmin's oppressions.

Learn, critique and use research techniques withheld from wimmin in the past.

Institutionalize reflexiveness, self-criticism and accountability in the research process.

Stress theoretical development as well as methodological efficiency.

Empower Research By, For and About Wimmin:

Conduct liberating research which enables wimmin to speak about their own lives, e.g. publish the words of housewives, third world wimmin, lesbians, etc.

Specify the conditions of wimmin in all areas of sociological specialization (medicine, law, theory, race and ethnicity), not merely in marriage and family or sex roles.

Rotate the manual/theoretical work or incorporate it into one process rather than falsely dichotomizing work.

Acknowledge/recognize the importance of coding, interviewing, and similar activities, giving credit where it is appropriate.

Recognize the importance of teaching as a dialogue That empowers students, and expands our own understanding, even though few rewards are offered by the discipline.

Confront the Abuse of Language:

    Critique patriarchal language, theory and concepts.

    Use language that is non-exclusive, accessible and de-mystified.

    Eliminate English chauvinism by incorporating bilingualism in journals, abstracts, course syllabi, and so forth.

    Stress the active voice instead of the passive voice.

Bypass Gatekeepers and Create New Forms of Feminist Criticism:

    Improve access to sociological/feminist conferences through sliding fees, accessible language, recruitment of community participants.

    Improve access to journals in the same manner: recruit non-academic research reviews, especially by groups who are "objects" of research; generate cross-disciplinary feminist reviews.

    Empower feminist ethics and feminist accountability in the development of feminist journals; create shared decision-making processes which involve boards and editors with more input from readers and the general public; change standards of excellence to include controversy, the goal of liberation and the importance of practice/reinvestment of research;

change reward structures to emphasize public
recognition of feminist accomplishments;
institutionalize the rotation of
even feminist gatekeeping positions.

Support feminists in the discipline(s) by passing on
knowledge, rather than withholding and creating a new
scarce resource.

Create inclusive feminist support/study groups.

Become feminist mentors who open the field to new
scholarship and new politics and new methods to
empower all wimmin.

Generate alternate forms of professional recognition,
scholarship and evaluation

These guidelines for a feminist ethic in the social sciences are not a completed mandate, but a responsible attempt to formulate rules for moral action.

ACKNOWLEDGMENT

We wish to thank Julia Penelope, Cynthia Trainor, Judy McCubbin, Sharon Selvage and Carole Kokes for their encouragement and support. We also note that the Collective typed and edited the entire final manuscript to reduce publication costs to our readers.

The Deep Structure of Gender Antithesis: Another View of Capitalism and Patriarchy

Dorothy E. Smith

Reflexive Statement

I have been active in the women's movement for quite a while and have wanted as a feminist to break down the barriers between the academic and the political. I'm a sociologist so I've wanted a sociology which would provide a feminist understanding of the large-scale political and economic relations and processes which shape our lives as women. Though I agree with many of the feminist criticisms of Marxism, I have also seen in Marxism a source of understanding which feminists can use without necessarily buying into the sexism. My thinking about patriarchy and capitalism has been focussed on how gender oppression has become part of class oppression. This doesn't mean reducing gender oppression to class oppression, but trying to see how they are related. The women's movement has more to say and more to struggle against than the issues with which we've identified the women's movement, important as they are. We have things to say about the society, about the economy and the political process and our specific issues are directly or indirectly tied into these. The critique of our oppression is a critique of patterns of exercising power in our societies; and I want to understand them better.

As our investigation of the moral worlds of women and men has developed, oppositions and contrasts have come into view. These gender antitheses are expressed in the context of feminist political organization, of the peace movement, of discussions of rationality in the context of philosophy, of psychological studies of moral development and where women in the women's movement talk about the moral and political differences between women and men. They differ from context to context. Yet each seems to bear upon the same underlying contrast between men's and women's modes of being, practices and experience in the contemporary world. In the context of the politics of the women's movement we have made a critique of male strategies of organization. We have come to suspect hierarchical relations of authority in which the few appropriate the effort and activity of the many and impose their will upon them. We have sought forms of organization which make it possible for each one to play her part and to speak to her interests and concerns in the enterprise[1]. In cultural and political contexts, we have been ambivalent about the ideologically constructed contrast between the male personality as rational, impersonal, objective, unemotional and the female personality as non- or ir-rational, intuitive, subjective, emotional and particularizing, seeing it at once as a dichotomy which charts our powerlessness and as detaching us from the problematics of the impersonal exercise of power. Philosophers have called into question a conception of rationality peculiarly identified with men (Cf. Harding, 1982:2-3), proposing that an alternative account of rationality is needed, unbound from the gender organization tying it into structures of power. Similarly it is suggested that an ethical stance grounded in impersonal principles has a gender subtext and that women's ethical judgments consider the presence and situation of the subject and her orientation to particular others (Cf. Gilligan, 1982:21).

In our most essential social medium, language, the social medium of feeling as well as rationality, of struggle as well as of oppression, feminist critics have addressed the exclusion of women and women's experience.[2] The problem of how to speak as women when discourse is fundamentally masculine and provides no medium for the expression of women's being has been posed.[3] We have asserted the standpoint of the experiencing individual situated in the everyday world. Thought, art and inquiry beginning from the "center" of an embodied consciousness has been conceived by feminists as the radical ground of the intellectual and artistic enterprise of women.[4]

These feminist antitheses are situated variously in the political and academic discourses of the contemporary world. But they betray common themes. They are, perhaps, most poignantly and powerfully expressed in the peace movement (Cf. Mooney in D. Thompson, 1983). They speak of an alienation from forms of power vested in rationality and abstraction; of ambivalence about the exercise of power; of a standpoint for women in the everyday world of their work; of a world of particular others and places in which there is love and hate, childbirth, sickness, death, and caring; of a subject situated in herself rather than in an alienated abstracted mode; of a sense of the particular connectedness of the world in contrast to destructive rationalities.

These themes arise in an experience of the world which is of our time, product of an historical process and committing us to the trajectory of our future. Though, as Harding (1982:2-3) points out, the dichotomy between male as rational, female as emotional has a history going back at least to Greece, in that society rationality was not identified with power. In our time, however, power and rationality are united in a ruling apparatus, a complex of administrative, managerial and professional organizations, interpenetrated by discursive relations. It is an organization of class coordinating and regulating the social process in relation to the complex organization of capital accumulation.

The ruling apparatus is constructed organizationally on principles of universality and impersonality. Its systems of rules, categories and administrative practices are in principle indifferent to the particularities of gender and gender relations. For the most part our thinking in the women's movement has addressed the visible predominance of men as a deviation from such principles resulting from bias and discrimination. Women would be treated equally in law, in business, in jobs, etc. were it not for distortions of rational process created by the operation of male chauvinism—so we have believed. But the deeper our analysis, the better our knowledge of history, the longer our experience of the sources and modes of resistance to change, the more visible is the gender subtext of the impersonal and universal forms of ruling.

This gender subtext concealed beneath apparently impersonal forms, is integral not contingent to the ruling apparatus. Gender roles and relations are not tucked away in those zones called sexuality, the family, interpersonal relations, etc. which are defined residually by the organization of paid work and the institutions of the ruling apparatus. In our phase of the long struggle of women for their emancipation, the political conception of patriarchy addresses forms of male dominance specific to this kind of society, not some abstract notion of male dominance as a property of societies across history, geography and cultural variation. The concept identifies, as Millett and Eisenstein make clear, not the private alone, but the private and public dominance of men. While Millett addresses the forms of dominance in sexual relations between women and men, she also locates patriarchy in the institutions of government, business, the military and the media--in short, what I am describing as a ruling apparatus. Similarly, Eisenstein identifies patriarchy with the hierarchical structures of power. Both indict the fundamentally patriarchal character of the ruling apparatus (Millett, 1971; Eisenstein, 1979).

The dynamic basis of the ruling apparatus lies in the separation of producers from the means of production, which also differentiates knowledge, judgment and will as distinct organizational functions. Marx describes a progressive process of transfer of these functions from individual craftsmen, peasant or artisan, to "the workshop as a whole." They become concentrated in the capital which employs workers and makes over "the intellectual potencies of the material process of production" (Marx, 1967:361). The capitalist who represents the collective will of the enterprise "makes science a productive force distinct from labour and presses it into the service of capital" (Marx, 1967:361).

The intensive and systematic development of the functions of knowledge, judgment and will as properties of organization rather than of individuals has been central in the emergence and elaboration of the ruling apparatus. In ways analogous to how the new productive processes of capital appropriated skills and knowledge from the peasant and craftsman, capital displaced, absorbed and expropriated the traditional skills and knowledge of women (Smith, 1983). This transfer accelerated as the nascent ruling apparatus emerged in the late 19th century. It included both the absorption of women's traditional skills, such as spinning or dairying into an industrial process dominated by men (Pinchbeck, 1969), or into the professional process -- for example, the attack by physicians on the folk traditions of midwives (Cf. Oakley, 1976; Donnison, 1977), and the active management of women's lives in the family through welfare systems, ideologies of child development, public health, etc.[5].

The changes precipitated by the rise of capitalism did not bring rationality into being, nor its appropriation by men, nor the male-enforced exclusion of women. But with capitalism rationality emerges as a specialized and discrete arena of action, of organizing and of exercising power. This is concurrent with a radical change in the relationships of women and men, and in the ways in which the gender division of labour situates the two sexes in the world (though it did not radically transform the gender division of labour as such) (Clark,1919).

Capitalism created a wholly new terrain of social relations external to local contexts and the particularities of traditional personally-mediated economic and social relations. It created an extra-local medium of activity constituted by a market process in which a multiplicity of anonymous buyers and sellers interrelate and by what Clark describes as "the mechanical state" (Clark, 1919), the state divorced from the persons and personalities of its rulers and vested in the impersonal operations of bureaucratic forms. These extra-local, impersonal, universalized forms of action became the exclusive terrain of men, while women became correspondingly confined to a reduced local sphere of action organized by particularistic relationships. As capitalism evolves into its monopoly form, this new arena enlarges and becomes increasingly organized by an apparatus of ruling, a complex division of labour among management, the state in its many aspects, the media and other textual discourses, professions and professional organizations, an expanding universe of action within abstraction. It is a terrain which has created new forms of action, new powers and potentialities for men.

Women's working lives have had a special relation to this order. For of course though men might dwell in abstractions as their mode of action, they exist also in bodily modes, in the world and are subject therefore in ordinary ways to needs for maintenance, for sexuality, food, comfort. There is a corresponding work in the abstracted mode which organizes its material environment to accommodate the specialized activity of the male, providing for the maintenance of the local environment and for the particularities of individual needs. Women's socialization and working experience has been and continues still to a large extent to be organized in the world of the local, the everyday, oriented towards the home, towards particular individuals and towards children. The ideology of gender orders, organizes and expresses the relations between the ruling apparatus as the arena of male activity and the work of women which has supported and sustained it.

The gender antitheses which we have described are located in the social relations organizing these two modes of being and their working relationships. That women have been identified with particularized relationships, with intuition, feeling, irrationality and subjectivity has not been merely as a contrastive exercise. Characterizations of masculinity and femininity reflect at the level of person and personality the relations of the ruling apparatus and the supporting ancillary work of women. Men are specifically trained to function in a world of work in which the calculative relations of the market process, the impersonal, rule-governed practices of bureaucracies, loyalty to impersonal organizations and so forth, must prevail over particularized relationships, personal feelings, and diffuse rather than functionally specific modes of action. Training is reinforced by a gender ideology which defines masculinity in contrast to its corresponding negative, the feminine.

The ruling apparatus vests activity, power, telos in forms of organization external to the individual. The individual comes to exercise power and initiative by virtue of his participation in these organizational and discursive forms. The ideology of masculinity and the socialization practices which incorporate it into the practices of men's being sever the individual's relation to those aspects of his being which connect him with particular others, as someone embodied, existing in a local world. Sustaining masculine ideology as a mode of being is a moral exercise. But if it is to be convincing as a mode of being, it must exist in settings and social relationships which are at least congruent with and at best reinforce it. It means that the individual's daily practices must contain him within a socially organized practice which detaches him from the world of particularized relationships and particular places as the focus of his thought and care. The gender division of labour does this work. Having assigned to woman the responsibility for the local and the particular, it seals off the masculine consciousness from involvements which would distract from servicing and performing the externalized relations of power in which men are both actor and instrument.

Underlying the impersonal and universalizing practices of the ruling apparatus are the processes of the self-expansion of capital which it for the most part serves. The interests which it in general serves have an uneasy and contradictory relation to the interests of those who service it. A disjuncture arises between the activity of individuals within the ruling apparatus and their local experience of themselves and others as particular private persons. Though for men active in the ruling apparatus, it represents an arena of expanded powers, fundamentally for most those powers are not theirs. They are the "employed," that is, the "used." If we scrutinize the detail of the workings of that world, we find that masculinity as an ideology operates on these contradictions, cutting men off from dimensions of their being through which they might be located in the actualities of their local and particular worlds, tying off the connections through which the life-blood of conviction might drain away from abstracted modes of action.

The extreme is the uses of masculinity as an ideology to form the fighting man as a mere instrument so that he can function as a component of a military machine committed to enterprises given the gloss of patriotism but serving interests and powers in which he has no part. The Marine, for example, learns to name those aspects of his being identified as weak, as feeling, as inwardly opposed to killing and the infliction of pain, as feminine, as the characteristics of a lower order of being to be repudiated in his self (Roberts, 1983). Homophobia among men is a fear of the feminine within created by this ideological practice. Its alienative structure can be seen equally clearly in accounts of the macho conduct of foreign affairs under Kissinger's leadership--for example his appraisal of the capacity of one man to work against his conscience on the planning of the Cambodian invasion as an exercise "separating the men from the boys" (Hersh,1983: 190). The same masculine ideology is at work in the approval of capacities to think and talk of megadeaths as the outcome of a nuclear war and to estimate the possibilities of a winnable nuclear war. The ideology of masculinity operates as a means of separating the individual from his conscience, qualms and sense of shared humanity, subordinating him to the raw pursuit of power and advantages in the interests of powers beyond him which are dimly seen, where the payoff is the jubilant exercise of power itself and the gender organization of its social acknowledgement in the respect of men and the sexual interest of women. A masculine ideology informs the identification of patriotism with the confrontational politics of rank power represented now in the speeches with which Reagan seeks to secure the consent of the American people to the military imposition of an imperialist will. An ideology instructing men to be strong, to be cool, to be hard, to compete, to conquer, to dedicate themselves to enterprises which are not theirs and to set aside considerations involving particular people, constructs them as agents of a ruling apparatus which serves the interests of expanding capital.

The critical antitheses of feminism have these relations as their historical site. Women are a social category outside or marginal to the ruling apparatus having a divergent consciousness, a different and opposing experience, situated in a different kind of work and different modes of relating, not wholly claimed by the seductive possibilities of power it offers.

Capitalism is deeply contradictory. It has a greater capacity for productivity than any other mode of production the world has so far seen. At the same time as its ruling practices create the threat of nuclear war, of administrative fascism, of ecological damage beyond any before, and poverty on a scale the world has never seen before, it has also made possible control of our environment, of disease, and of poverty as never before. It is the same with the ruling apparatus itself. Its medium is in writing and print and telecommunications. Its forms of knowledge, communication, organization and action are mediated by "texts." These are modes of relating which are extra-local, which have proved capable of creating relations on a different basis than ever before, which release people from the confinement, the deadly narrowness, the enforced conformities of the local community of old. Though these media of speaking and acting have been progressively preempted by the ruling apparatus they are not essentially so.

These contradictions are the site of women's struggles. In the 19th century women explored an expanded relation to the world through writing and print. They fought for knowledge, for higher education, for the right to political presence. Now a new and more radical phase of that struggle has been entered. The critique of male practices of rationality, hierarchy and domination described earlier claims an access for women to the media of textual communication, action and relation. They create a base in the 'enemy territory' for a discourse among women. The expansion and deepening of this discourse among women insert a new mode on the margins of the ruling apparatus proposing an alternative to the practices of ruling. It is not, of course, the only one. The racism and class oppression which capitalism has created are also bases of struggle. Nor are women alone in opposing the alienating powers of the ruling apparatus. We share the margins of struggle with others. But we come from a special place which has been historically and socially imposed on us. It gives us a base in the world from which we speak of the intimate, the ordinary, the personal. It no longer confines us as it once did (for the ideologies of gender sustaining the ruling apparatus also restricted the scope of the discourse of women). But we have seen the possibility of remaking the way in which speaking is done and in which power is exercised. We are attempting to create in the margins of the textually-mediated world a non-alienated consciousness, a non-alienated mode of political discourse. We are struggling to find new modes of understanding and changing the world, of speaking from and of particularity, from and of experience, from and of the everyday world, from and of the subject in herself, from and of the actualities of people's lives and relationships and to create ways of organizing preventing us from becoming merely a means to enterprises which endanger these actualities and <u>are not ours</u>.

NOTES

1. The well-known left-wing version of this issue is Sheila Rowbotham, Lynn Segal and Hilary Wainwright, *Beyond the Fragments: Feminism and the Making of Socialism* (London: Merlin Press), 1979.

2. See, among others, Dale Spender, *Man Made Language* (London: Routledge and Kegan Paul), 1980.

3. Most powerfully by French feminist thinkers. See, for example Helene Cixous, "The laugh of the medusa," in Elizabeth Abel and Emily K. Abel (eds) *The SIGNS Reader: Women, Gender and Scholarship.* (Chicago: University of Chicago Press), 1983, pp 279-297.

4. For example, Dorothy E. Smith, "A sociology for women," in J. Sherman and E.T. Beck (eds) *The Prism of Sex: Essays in the Sociology of Knowledge* (Madison: University of Wisconsin Press), 1979; Lucy Lippard, *From the Centre: Feminist Essays on Women's Art* (New York), 1973; Nancy Hartsock, "Feminist theory and the development of revolutionary strategy," in Zillah R. Eisenstein (ed) *Capitalist Patriarchy and the Case of Socialist Feminism* (New York: Monthly Review Press), 1979; Suzanne Juhasz, *Naked and Fiery Forms: Modern American Poetry by Women: A New Tradition* (New York), 1976.

5. See Jane Lewis, *The Politics of Motherhood* (London: Croom Helm), 1981; Jacques Donzelot, *The Policing of Families* (New York: Pantheon Books), 1979; and others.

Researching Prostitution: Some Problems for Feminist Research

Carol Smart

Reflexive Statement

Carol Smart is currently researching drug addiction at the Institute of Psychiatry, The University of London. From 1979 to 1982 she was research fellow at the Centre for Criminological and Socio-Legal Studies at the University of Sheffield and prior to that was Lecturer in Sociology for four years at Trent Polytechnic, Nottingham. She now lives in London, is a committed feminist and her main interests are in law and women's position in the family.

Introduction

Prostitution has been an important political issue for feminists in the United Kingdom for over a century. In the middle of the nineteenth century it was the focus of a long-running campaign whose central figure was Josephine Butler. At that time the feminists and their supporters were fighting against the extremely repressive Contagious Diseases Acts which allowed the authorities to forcibly imprison and examine any woman thought to be a prostitute and which created a register of women subject to intensive police surveillance (Walkowitz, 1980). More recently, prostitution has been raised as a political issue by PROS (Programme for the Reform of the Laws on Soliciting) and by the ECP (English Collective of Prostitutes). The PROS campaign has concentrated on the abolition of imprisonment for prostitutes with the longer-term goal of complete decriminalisation, while the ECP has focused more on the economic exploitation of women and the specific legal harassment of prostitute women.

A main feature which has united feminists across all these generations has been an outrage over the laws on soliciting and prostitution. Although prostitute women suffer a multiplicity of disadvantages and oppression, the criminal law is, and has been, both the epitome of those oppressions and their major source. These laws have not only criminalised a section of women who are already exploited through low wages and who are particularly vulnerable to physical and sexual violence, but operate a double standard which ensures that, almost exclusively, it is women who carry the blame and the consequences of prostitution. Moreover, in the UK, the laws on soliciting and loitering for the purposes of prostitution apply only to women and simultaneously deny those women the usual civil rights accorded to anyone who is accused of a criminal offence.

An understanding of the law in this area and a recognition of its far-reaching effects has therefore been a major concern of feminists and has led to a range of studies from Walkowitz's (1980) scholarly, historical research, to Jaget's (1980) collection of the experiences of French prostitutes up against the law, to the London Borough of Camden's own research in 1983 on police/women relations in the so-called red light district of King's Cross. However, in spite of this background of much feminist research on prostitution, certain problems remain for feminists who are working in the area. Although these problems are not peculiar to the issue of prostitution, they are particularly acute here and raise questions which must be addressed before feminist research progresses much further.

Problems Facing Feminist Research

The first major ethical problem facing the researcher is whether prostitution remains a feminist issue. Of course on one level it is possible to say that everything under the sun is a feminist issue because it must in some form eventually affect women. But this is no real answer because what the question implies is whether concentrating on the issue of prostitution is not in fact ultimately detrimental to women. Given that the purpose of much recent work carried out in this area has been to reveal the oppressive nature of the law it might seem hard to understand how this could worsen the oppression of women. But we must take on board this argument because if a feminist emphasis on the way in which the law discriminates against prostitute women merely produces new legislation to criminalise clients then all we achieve is an equality of misery. Furthermore, if we succeed in changing the law, such that there are no adverse legal consequences attached to prostitution, are we not simply condoning an unrestricted sexual exploitation of women? This argument is particularly acute when we recognise that the relationship between prostitute and client--where he has the economic power to "buy" her, to make her submit to his demands, and to celebrate his masculine sexuality--is the absolute antithesis of feminist goals. Of course the major flaw in this argument is that the current law does not restrict prostitution to any great extent as it mainly seeks to control street prostitution and not other forms. The law is also, in effect, just another burden for prostitute women to bear. Moreover the law on prostitution affects *all* women in that it presumes to divide us into categories of sexually respectable and unrespectable and thereby perpetuates an oppressive double standard.

But an issue remains and that is whether research in this area, attached as it is to certain political reforms, deflects from long-term feminist goals. This question can of course equally be posed of research on marriage. Does, for example, research on the failure of men to support their wives financially, lead to pressure for reforms which may improve the status of wives yet make marriage, which remains an oppressive institution, more "popular" with women? Ultimately this problem must be resolved by distinguishing between long and short-term objectives. Feminists cannot ignore the effects and the consequences of law as it operates in the present, so I would argue that to concentrate on research in this area is indeed a valuable feminist enterprise. In the long term, however, prostitution can only "wither away" if women's bodies cease to be commodities, with an economic value, and when women can earn reasonable wages working in other jobs. This of course entails working for such goals as more jobs, better wages and more nurseries which will benefit *all* women. Concentrating efforts, be they academic or political, on specific issues such as prostitution does not mean that we are insensitive to the dilemmas it poses.

It simply means that we cannot ignore the kind of treatment that is given to prostitutes in the present in favour of working towards an intangible sexual revolution in the distant future.

If doing research on prostitution can be justified from a feminist position this does not mean that there are no further problems to be encountered. An important one is, of course, the relationship between feminist research per se and feminist politics. This is an extremely complex issue which has spawned a great deal of debate (Stanley and Wise, 1983; Roberts, 1981; McRobbie, 1982) and which continues to be unresolved. I do not have space to engage with this debate, which is in any case well documented elsewhere. Here, rather, I wish to turn to the problems facing a feminist who has decided to do research, and in particular research on prostitution.

There has already been a considerable amount of research carried out on prostitution (Henriques, 1968; Glover, 1969; Davis, 1971; Greenwald, 1970; Bryan, 1973). The inadequacy of this work has been documented elsewhere (Smart, 1976) but the main thrust of existing research has been to concentrate on the woman who works as a prostitute rather than on prostitution as an institution which reflects the oppression of women. As a consequence prostitute women have been pathologised. Either they have been seen as the deviants or as pathetic and simple-minded victims. Clearly, no feminist would want to add to this type of literature, either wittingly or unintentionally. For this reason, when I started my research on prostitution, I took the decision that my focus would not be prostitute women because enough had been written on the women. What is more, even relatively sympathetic material always seemed to become voyeuristic and damaging to the women involved (e.g., Winn, 1974). I decided therefore to study both the law and agents of the law who dispensed "justice," or more usually punishment, to prostitute women. In the UK, prostitutes appear before magistrates who are predominately lay justices who are selected for office because of their work in the community. Magistrates can be considered to be amongst the "locally powerful" (Bell, 1978) because not only do they dispense the law but they are frequently local business *men* and employers or the wives of such worthies.

This decision to study the locally powerful posed a new category of problems for trying to do feminist research. Much of what is written on developing such work (e.g., Oakley, 1981) concentrates on how inadequate traditional methods and practices are when applied to the study of women or women's issues. A feminist ethic has developed which insists that feminist researchers not treat women simply as interview fodder or objects of research. Having recognised that the interviewer or researcher is in a relatively powerful position vis-a-vis the researched, feminists are trying to even out this power imbalance by sharing information with women and involving them more in the purpose of the research. The need to do this has been shown particularly forcefully by Oakley's research on pregnancy where she became a major source of support for a lot of the pregnant women in her sample.

These ethics of feminist research are unimpeachable, but they do not help a feminist who is doing research on the locally powerful who are predominently men. Arguably it is important for feminists to study "upwards" rather than "sideways" or more traditionally "downwards" toward the disadvantaged. But if we do, we find that the new tenets of research do not help us a great deal. For example the basic assumption that the researcher is in a more powerful position than the researched does not always hold good when the researcher is a woman and the researched are well-established and frequently, in their own terms, important men. Such people are not afraid to refuse to answer questions or to tell you what they think of your research, or ultimately to terminate the interview at their convenience. Of course the researcher retains the power of being able to go away and write up the research as she sees fit but this practice is also one which is currently being criticised by feminists. For example, Stanley and Wise (1983) have argued that the researcher should display her actions, reasonings, deductions and evidence to other people, and they argue that,

> If *they* are vulnerable, then *we* must be prepared to show ourselves as vulnerable too (Stanley and Wise, 1983:181).

What Stanley and Wise appear to overlook, however, is that it is feminists who are vulnerable, whether in the academy or other areas of life, and that making ourselves even more vulnerable by discussing our reasoning and purposes to those we research is not *always* a useful policy. Certainly Stanley and Wise are right when they argue that we as researchers owe some responsibility to the researched, whether we morally approve of them or not, but powerful groups like the police, the judiciary, the banks and so on, are quite capable of resisting our attempts to research them without us making ourselves more vulnerable to them. In the UK, where access to institutions such as the police, courts and judges is very difficult to achieve, announcing oneself as a feminist would almost certainly mean the end of one's research project.

The current writing on the ethics of feminist research has fallen into the presumption that feminists will only study women. Even those who do not make this assumption, such as Stanley and Wise, nonetheless presume we will study the relatively powerless or stigmatised groups in society such as men in prison or male sexual "deviants." Although these men may be powerful vis-a-vis individual women they have little power in the social order as a whole. So we need to start to think of ways to study the powerful and to consider whether, in these cases, feminism can direct us towards research and of course inform our analysis. However, the application of a feminist approach to research processes still has little to say about the ethics of actually doing the research.

This was certainly my experience when I interviewed magistrates about prostitution and the law. I realised very quickly that there would be value in discussing, with most of the magistrates, my reasoning and purpose. Consider for example the following quotations from magistrates.

> "Oh yes, unquestionably (soliciting should be a criminal offense). There are many reasons. Number one is that it's a form of obscenity which is offensive to the ordinary respectable citizen. And secondly

it's a temptation to foolish men, usually in drink, to waste their money and perhaps contract venereal disease."

"Very often I think they're lazy, they don't want regular work, and many start almost straight from school...There's a sort of friendship amongst them of course but I think they find it an easy way of getting money."

"I think the jail sentence...is a good thing you know, because if they are really bad prostitutes and don't look after themselves it's a way of them being at least examined now and again."

"I think that detectives in the vice squad are so very familiar with this problem that they would never put that sort of handle on a woman who was anything near decent, you know."

Even the magistrates who did not regard prostitute women as a despised social group who were morally and physically diseased tended to speak of the women as "these people." They may have had sympathy but prostitute women were always perceived as a segregated social group, to be separated from normal, respectable women.

Besides experiencing the futility of attempting to challenge such views or even of offering an alternative perspective in the interview situation, my major concern in doing this form of research became a fear that in giving magistrates the opportunity to vent their sexist views unchallenged, I was condoning and perhaps reinforcing the ideological oppression of women. A real dilemma presented itself in which I could either listen to frequently extremely objectionable comments on women who were prostitutes (but which contained an oppressive message for <u>all</u> women including myself) or terminate the research. I chose the former option but at considerable personal cost and with continuing intellectual doubts. Ultimately, I reasoned that my collusion with such blatant sexism probably harmed me more than the purpose of feminism. I can now reveal after all the views of a sample of magistrates on prostitute women, and by extension <u>all</u> women, and arguably that is a valuable exercise. I am not certain, however, what this means for the ethics of doing such research. Certainly my feminist principles were compromised, although realistically we must realise that our principles are frequently compromised. My experience was certainly no worse than what many feminists experience on a daily basis if they wish to keep their jobs. Moreover if we decide that it is important to study such subjects as the views of the police on rape, or the ideological position of the judiciary on women offenders, we cannot then abandon the project because their statements offend our feminist principles, or, because of the personal distress. In the final analysis we need to recognise that there is no ideal-type of feminist research which will remain true to a unified feminist ethic. The methods and practices we employ when interviewing the powerful must be different from those employed with women, or feminist research will become trapped into a perpetual study of women's powerlessness and will fail to adequately address the mechanisms of power most frequently (although not exclusively) exercised by men.

Lesbian Research Ethics

Pauline Bart

Reflexive Statement

As a casualty of the fifties, one of those legions of women who lived "The American Dream" in the suburbs, and found it a nightmare, I know how important feminism is for the lives of all women. When I returned to the school where I had obtained my M.A. at 31 (UCLA), and received my Ph.D. at 37, no one was interested in hiring me. I was "too old to be an assistant professor" and my dissertation was about an irrelevant group, depressed middle-aged women (or "Portnoy's Mother's Complaint"). While I have held positions at three universities and been a visiting professor at two, I have never had a "real" position in a department of Sociology, which may be why I have not been coopted.

This is the first academic or quasi-academic piece I have written specifically dealing with lesbian issues. It is not on my Vita because of homophobia. My recent research has focussed on violence against women, notably rape avoidance and pornography. Previously I worked on issues regarding women's health. Catharine MacKinnon's statement that "It is the unexceptionality of the victimization of women that is the hallmark of feminist theory" informs my work. I am a poet, like to do poetry readings and belong to the Feminist Writers Guild as well as the ASA, SSSP and NWSA, etc.

Lesbian Research Ethics

As one who agrees with Mencken, that "every profession is a conspiracy against the public," I have always been wary of codes of professional ethics. As a radical feminist, I have come to understand that being called "unprofessional" means that the men don't do it, e.g., embroider at meetings or be a pregnant attorney in court. As a lesbian I wonder "Why are these ethics different from any other ethics?" as the question, "Why is this night different from every other night?" is asked at Passover seders.

I believe the purpose of feminist research is to demystify the world for women. We in the Women's Movement believe that the personal is the political, so that how we live our personal lives is also a political act. I once stated, "Just because you sleep with women at night doesn't mean you can screw them during the day" and ended a poem:

> Facism starts with treating the first woman
>   as a means
> Not an end
> Discarding her like a used kleenex
> How you treat every woman is a political act
> All the rest is mere elaboration.

Lesbian ethics are feminist ethics plus. For example, the title of this article uses the word, "lesbian," rather than some euphemism such as "woman identified" (not all lesbians ARE woman identified and many non-lesbians do not understand its use as code). By daring to use the term "lesbian" I am not participating in the maintenance of the invisibility of lesbians in phallocentric thinking. Frye (1983: 156) notes that the Oxford English Dictionary states that lesbian is an adjective that means "of or pertaining to the island of Lesbos," and has an entry describing at length and favorably an implement called a lesbian rule..."a device used by carpenters. Period."

Are lesbian research ethics written by lesbians, or ethics derived from lesbian feminist principles, or ethics about how lesbians should behave in relationships with other lesbians? Lesbians have written from each of these positions. For example, Marcia Freedman, founding mother of the Israeli feminist movement, has written "Four Essays in Morality" (unpublished) which bases her morality on the model of a nurturant mother-child relationship (see her article in Beck, 1982).

How lesbians should behave towards one another was discussed at a National Women's Studies Association meeting (1983) and reported in Off Our Backs (1983). The assumption underlying this discussion was that "being a lesbian is more than sexual preference." I would add that being a lesbian researcher is more than being a good researcher.

Turning to the issue of researching lesbians, first I will highlight some particularly important ethical issues. Then I will present a case of a heterosexual woman researching lesbians who, with the Chair of her committee, violated every canon of lesbian research ethics.

(1) The first principle of lesbian research ethics is to recognize the importance of confidentiality. People's jobs and relationships with their families are at stake and their identities should be protected at all costs if that is their wish.

(2) It is important to be honest about who you are. It is unethical to pass as straight, bisexual or lesbian when engaging in research.

(3) It is particularly important to get feedback and share the results with the women you are studying, especially if you are heterosexual or bisexual, or if you are a lesbian, but primarily live in a different subculture from the one you are studying; for example, if you are a lesbian feminist and are studying women in butch-femme or stud-lady roles. (This is of course not very different from feminist research ethics, but the salience of point one is greater and the second point is more relevant.)

A Specific Analysis of Ethics and Lesbian Research

In 1972 a heterosexual woman asked me to chair her proposed dissertation on urban lesbian couples. Since heterosexual women could no more study lesbians in 1972 than whites could study Blacks during the era of Black nationalism, I refused, telling her it could not be done. I agreed to be on her committee but not to chair it. When she predictably blundered in her research as well as in a talk to a class on the sociology of deviance at another university, the community lesbian newspaper headlined an article "Beware of the Researcher" and warned lesbians not to talk to her.

In response to this article (because I was concerned that this meant that only women with "no politics" would talk with her) a meeting was arranged at a church which was attended by the researcher, the chair of her committee, myself and about five members of the lesbian community, including two who had heard her talk. The lesbians agreed to provide her with subjects and she agreed to show them what she wrote, and incorporate the feedback they would give her into her dissertation. I taped the meeting.

She conditionally failed her field exams, passing only after redoing two questions and answering a third about lesbian mothers, since she had demonstrated an ignorance of their existence. Her lesbian couple proposal was circulated and responded to by two lesbian psychologists and two lesbian sociologists. At her hearing on the proposal it was clear that she had not kept her word about incorporating the feedback, and so I failed her while the other members, all male, passed her. I was then taken off her committee but was never notified of that fact. However, other committee members, including one from another university, were given that information.

Apparently, on the assumption that I had left for the SSSP/ASA meetings in San Francisco, a notice and the dissertation were put in my box stating that the defense of the dissertation was going to be held during the ASA meetings (presumeably so I wouldn't know I was off the committee). I unsuccessfully tried to have the defense postponed but since at this point I was told that since I was not on the committee there was little I could do. The lesbian feedback group which had spent much time and energy critiquing her work justifiably felt that they had been had.

The dissertation fortunately was an intellectual but not a political disaster. However, as one of the lesbians giving feedback predicted, the dissertation was published as a book, even though the chair of her committee had promised it would not be.

A sociology department would be suspicious of a dissertation done by a white student on Blacks if s/he removed all the Black members from her/his committee. However, this did not occur when Ms. X made her Committee frauenfree (although one woman she had removed was asked by the departmental chair to be present at the defense).

This furnishes a prime example of unethical behavior in research on lesbians, not only by the researcher, but by her dissertation committee, one of whose members considered the agreement with the lesbian community censorship. There clearly was collusion involved between at least some of the men and the researcher.

This case demonstrates the need for codification of ethics in researching stigmatized groups, and sanctions when these ethics are violated. A participant in the lesbian community group that negotiated with Ms. X in the church and who also was in the academic lesbian feedback group was a member of the recent American Sociological Association Ethics Committee. She made sure that the revised code of ethics contained provisions explicitly preventing what happened in Ms. X's case to occur again without sanctions.

NOTES

1. This latter example was provided by Catharine MacKinnon.

2. For example, she states that violence is not an ethic for the gynocracies, unless necessary for the defense of one's self or children. Nature and Life are seen organically rather than hierarchically stratified.

3. Because I have been on doctoral committees at universities other than the one where I presently teach, it should not be assumed this took place at the University of Illinois.

On the Ethics of Research on the Triple Oppression of Black American Women

Linda Williams

Reflexive Statement

I am a 37-year-old black American woman. Like many black women of my generation, I participated in the "Civil Rights" and "Black Power" struggles. By the early 1970s I also turned my attention to the overarching functions of class exploitation in the United States. While I believed myself to be "automatically" concerned about the problems and rights of women as well, my real energies, both in theory and praxis, were directed almost exclusively to issues of race and class. Meanwhile, the feminization of poverty and black women's deeper suffering within the ranks of the poor grew. The dissolution of black family life continued, and, despite the "myth of the superwoman," black women remained the worst off group according to most major social indicators. Ultimately objectively deteriorating conditions for black women pierced my consciousness and turned my attention to the need for scholarly research into the plight of black American women in light of the capitalist political economy of the United States in the post World War II era. This essay elaborates three themes: the state of research on black women, the present situation of black women, and the need for a new politics reflecting the realities of black American women's triple oppression.

Introduction

Major changes have occurred in the black female occupational structure. Most notable are the decline of black females as agrarian workers and urban domestics, their incorporation into the clerical and professional strata, and the income gains among black females relative to white females. But these developments, registered in the changing occupational composition of the labor force in the United States and the deteriorating income structure of white women, have occurred in a manner that has not eliminated black women's inequality, but instead has reproduced it in a new setting.

The persistence of black women's inequality is particularly striking because of the strong forces (e.g., urban and northern migration, political practices, civil rights laws and policies, etc.) working in recent decades to equalize black and white incomes as well as male and female incomes in the United States. The persistence of inequality between black women and other groups in the face of such pressures poses a major anomaly for conventional explanation of racial and sexual inequality.

Clearly more scholarly research is needed to confront the reified images of black women and clarify the conditions, causes of the conditions, and political responses to the conditions of black women. This chapter makes a contribution to a better understanding of the socio-economic and political experiences of black American women in the post World War II era.

While no fully developed alternative theoretical framework is presented, I explore the broad contours of an approach that places conflict, power, and collective activity as the starting points of its understanding of political and economic processes. This alternative theorization views the determination of income and job distribution as resulting both from market processes and processes of power and conflict between workers and capitalists. The organization of jobs and the fragmentation of consciousness become key variables in explaining the persistence of black female inequality.

The Importance of Studying Black Women

Several preliminary points can be made. First, the study of black women in all of its aspects is important. Approximately fourteen million Americans or 53 percent of all black people in the United States are female (U.S. Bureau of the Census, 1984). There can be no substantial improvements in the conditions of black Americans without fundamental positive changes in the experiences of over one-half the black population. Perhaps this is one of the reasons black women are a central part of the consistent leaders of the struggles of blacks for equality and human rights.

Second, black women play not only a specific and special role as mothers, but also as workers. Black women are essential providers much more often than are white women. Even when married, black women continue to work for wages outside the home at higher rates than white women do, supplementing the low wages generally paid to black males. For black women, it is clear that just getting a job outside the home may make women more independent, but it is not the essence of genuine liberation. Thus, understanding black women's experiences can contribute new insights to all women's struggles.

Third, the great majority of black women are not only blacks and females, but also members of the working class. To build working class unity, we must analyze the differences that divide as well as the common interests that bind different sectors of the oppressed. These differences are based not simply in socio-psychological subjective interests, but also in short-term material objective interests. The study of black women can elucidate differences and commonalities between fractions of the working class.

For these and other reasons the paucity of literature on black women is stunning. Nowhere is this scarcity more evident than in the major academic journals of the social sciences. For example, the index of the <u>American Political Science Review</u> reveals that since it began publishing in 1911 this prestigious journal has never carried an article on black women. Even scholarly journals on the left, such as <u>Politics and Society</u>, have failed to publish any articles on black women. Possibly the general lack of attention given to black women's issues in established academic circles helps explain why too many of the rare studies on black women must claim as their signal achievement the reinforcement of fictitious cliches. They have given credence to grossly distorted categories through which the black woman continues to be perceived.

For example, in the words of black political activists, in the 1960s and 1970s the black woman has been labeled "castrating female."[1] She has been advised: "What makes a woman appealing is femininity, and she can't be feminine without being submissive." At the founding convention of the Congress of African People held in Atlanta in September 1979, Bibi Amina Baraka set the tone for the series of black women workshops by advising black females to internalize "submitting to (their) natural roles" by studying their attitudes toward their "Man, house, and children."[2] Sisters need to take cooking classes, learn to create tasty recipes, and improve their personal hygiene. In her presentation on the black family, Akiba ya Elimu suggested that black males were the natural leaders of the black community in all social, cultural and political relations. Kasis Washao summarized the proceedings of the convention with a few appropriately sexist remarks: Black women should "be humble and loving, appreciative, and resourceful, faithful, respectful and understanding . . . to provide continuous inspiration for their husbands."

For white feminists, black women are simultaneously the quintessential victims of sexist oppression and the symbol of courageous, industrious womanhood. As Phyllis Palmer points out in her insightful essay on white women and black women,

> Black women, even more than other women forced to labor outside their homes, came to symbolize for feminists sexuality, prowess, mysterious power (mysterious, certainly, since it is so at odds with

their actual economic, political, and social deprivation) the "myth of the superwoman." (Palmer, 1983)

Most white women write and act as if they have staked out the common feminist ground, and that divergence from this is a diversionary "special interest." White feminist academics, in particular, formulate theories grounded in notions of universal female powerlessness in relation to men, and of women's deprivation relative to men's satisfaction. Often treating race and class as secondary factors in social organization, feminist theorists write from experiences in which race and class are not felt as oppressive elements in their lives. It is this theorizing from white, middle-class experience that contributes to the ethnocentrism often observed in white feminist writings (Simmons, 1979).

Just as the gender literature tends to omit race, the race literature gives little attention to women. Recently, the area of race relations inquiry has been dominated by debate over the relative importance of race or class in explaining the historical and contemporary status of blacks in the United States. Analysis of the interaction of race, sex, and class falls squarely between these two developing bodies of theoretical literature.

Other academic works on black women have been content to examine the history of black female and black male participation in the women's movement (Lerner, 1972; Flexner, 1975) or at worst, to expound the "black matriarchy" thesis (Moynihan, 1970). Conservative white male writers have fretted over the supposed image of the black female as an unworthy "double token" in the age of affirmative action (Glazer, 1978). Others, such as Reagan mentor George Gilder, have cast black women as willing proponents of the breakdown of the black family in order to receive welfare. According to Gilder, the matriarchal black family structure is the basic cause of continuing income differentials between black families and white families.

These are but a few of the common misconceptions, distortions, incomplete and wrong analyses that continue to plague the black woman. To go beyond these incorrect "analyses" of black female experiences in the United States, the forces that reproduce black women's inequality must be understood. To identify these forces, analysis of class conflict and markets is the proper starting point. Such an analysis demonstrates that market forces in American capitalism have not worked to eliminate the triple oppression of black women. Only economic and political pressure from black women allied principally with black men and also to a limited extent with white women and the labor movement has brought about minimal advances for black females.

What, then, are the prospects for black American women in the future? The final section briefly analyzes this question.

A "Feminist Ethic" for Black American Women: From Research to Practice

According to many economists, capital remains in the midst of a major economic crisis of accumulation. Many predicted another downturn at the end of 1984 (Washington Post, 1984). Without major policy changes, sectors of the private economy expected to do well in the mid and late 1980s include energy, high technology, and services (Business Week, June, 1981). Many human-service oriented corporations, especially in the fields of advertising, travel, banking, credit agencies, and insurance will expand. Others, such as public education, auto services, and so forth will contract sharply in the next years. Government employment, particularly in lower paid white-collar and blue-collar positions, will be reduced significantly (Business Week, June, 1981).

What will be the position of black female workers within the new capitalist economy if these conditions hold? On the one hand, and in general, black female workers, like all females, are more heavily concentrated in some growth areas than are black males--e.g., health services, finance, etc.--but only in the lower positions. On the other hand, black female employment in better positions--e.g., professional and managerial positions--is high only in declining sectors of the economy, particularly government employment. Black female unemployment is already high in these declining sectors. Market processes appear to offer little, if any, hope of improvement for black females.

Meanwhile, political forces are stacked against blacks and females in general. For example, the Equal Rights Amendment was defeated, and in 1984 the Supreme Court reinforced racism and sexism within unions by insisting that blacks and women must prove that seniority systems were designed to "intentionally discriminate" against them. By the 1980s much of the political terrain shifted to the right. White blue-collar workers voted strongly for Ronald Reagan in 1980, albeit not as strongly as affluent whites. The League of Revolutionary Black Workers, the Black Panther Labor caucuses and other revolutionary-oriented organizations within the black working class no longer existed. Ralph Abernathy and Hosea Williams, once strong Civil Rights politicians, supported Reagan's candidacy. An entire class of black farmers, sharecroppers, and rural laborers almost completely disappeared, eliminating part of the social foundation for the Civil Rights struggles in the Deep South a generation ago. As an activist in the Amalgamated Clothing Workers Union, Coleman Young led the creation of the fiercely independent National Negro Labor Council in the 1950s; years later, as mayor of Detroit, he forged a conservative political alliance with corporate capital at the expense of black and poor constituents.

Probably the greatest negative impact upon the material interest of black women and more generally all blacks, all women, all workers, is in the area of public policy. The massive spending reductions of the Reagan Administration are "racist" and "sexist" in that they have a disproportionately higher effect on blacks and women. Cuts in Aid for Dependent Children, medicaid, food stamps, child nutrition, and fuel assistance all hurt black women most who are disproportionately recipients of these programs. For example, in 1980, 21 percent of all black females were receiving public assistance and supplemental income transfers versus seven percent of black males, five percent of white females, and two percent of white males.

Clearly black women, the continuing victims of triple oppression, are most in need of encouragement and support in waging battles on class, racial, and sexual fronts. Fundamental advances will occur only when we can move beyond sexual, racial, and class divisions and into a class-wide movement. Yet, no working-class movement is on the horizon. Even within the separable but always interrelated spheres of oppression, capitalist market and political processes have structurally differentiated oppressed groups, making common struggles more difficult.

For example, polls have shown that while many working-class black women do not sympathize with the women's liberation movement as such, these same women respond affirmatively to specific feminist demands--such as equal pay, equal job opportunities, and equal legal rights. In their response to such specific demands, black women statistically have been the most feminist of all.

But historically the feminist movement has put forth solutions that only go half way. While white women have emphasized sexual oppression, and black women have tended to emphasize racial oppression over sexual oppression, neither has given much attention to class exploitation. Thus both are partially correct, and yet both do not go far enough. White women are correct in asserting that all female incomes remain low compared with all male incomes, and any women living as a sole income earner is likely to be precariously perched just above the poverty line. They are correct in asserting that the single white woman is likely to live on less income than the single black man. But black women are correct in asserting that the expectation of living on a single female income is much less pervasive or probable for white women. These __material__ differences between black female and white female experiences have led to different interest and policy foci: for instance, while white women have emphasized marriage and motherhood and fought against tax prices that disadvantage married couples, and fought for pension rights, black women have emphasized full employment, child-care, housing, and restructuring the welfare system.

Because of the accident of class position derived from association through daughterhood, wifehood, or sisterhood with various male relations, many white women have assumed that political and legal rights, and protection for women within the family were universally pre-eminent goals. Especially in the middle class, they have tacitly accepted degrees of economic dependence and have been unwilling to violate social forms, or to risk economic loss, by demanding that they be separately responsible for their economic support and separately accountable for their wage earnings. At the simplest level, many married, middle-class, white women have a choice about whether or not to work full-time for wages. They generally do not have to earn an equal or major portion of the income that provides their food, clothing, or shelter. In short, married, white, middle-class women do not usually have the primary responsiblity (and authority) that is derived from earning incomes equivalent to their husbands. Even in middle-class households where the wife is a full-time income earner, her income is substantially less than her husband's. Ironically, the higher the household income, the less important may be the wife's wages.

For working-class white as well as black families, a wife's income may be more essential than for a middle-class family, and yet the income itself is so low that working-class women are more aware of their continued need for their husbands' paychecks. The low wage available to white, working-class and black women, however, may have made them more reluctant to join a middle-class women's movement that seems more concerned with redistributing power within the family than challenging the powerlessness of women (and men) outside the home.

The essential fact--that for most women, economic well-being means attachment to a male wage earner--might have led middle-class, white women to join efforts with white working-class and with black women to increase their ability to earn income and to end the economic dependency that provides a material basis for male dominance. But white, middle-class women have the greatest dependence on male income, in the sense that their household incomes are highest because of it. Because their derived income is greatest, they have the least incentive to challenge their income dependence and to advocate the economic self-reliance of all women. In the long run, as divorce and separation statistics indicate, such women do not have a protected and guaranteed position; it is in their long-term interest to consider what their situations might be as single women. But to do so, to consider seriously the problems raised by single black women and working-class women who live with working-class white and black men, is to question the organization of a society in which "their" men fare better.

The necessity in the mid-1980s is to rethink both theory and praxis so that they incorporate race, class, and sex into a coherent comprehension of the life circumstances for varieties of women and men. Only then will all the oppressed and exploited be able to confront the challenge of the 1980s.

NOTES

1. Nathan and Julia Hare cite many of these cliches in their article "Black male-female relationships," Transaction, 7 (November-December, 1977).

2. These are the words of West Coast cultural nationalist Maulana Ron Karenga. Cited in Bonnie Dill, "Race, class, and gender: Prospects for an all inclusive sisterhood," Feminist Studies 9 (Spring): 131-150.

A Feminist Research Ethos

Ann R. Bristow and Jody A. Esper

Reflexive Statement

One of us was raped 12 years ago. We find that mainstream psychological and sociological literature fails to capture that experience. The positivist and masculinist social science model in which we were trained is inadequate in producing knowledge representative of the reality of women's lives. We have found the process and products of research to be inseparable, affirming what feminists have acknowledged in various settings, working on diverse tasks. What follows is an attempt to apply our feminist consciousness to the research process.

Introduction

A 41 year-old woman calls the office; she has seen announcements of our research project calling for volunteers--women who have experienced rape five or more years ago. "I don't know if I can help you, but I was raped 16 years ago, and only my husband knows." During a later, three and one-half hour conversation, she prefaces a description of her fears by saying that, "you're going to think I'm crazy but.. " She is answered by a woman who shares her own fears as a rape survivor and reveals that many of the women interviewed have expressed similar fears. She seems relieved. We wonder how much she has thought that we would sit in judgment of her.

The above description is part of a research process through which the longer-term effects of, and responses to, rape are being studied. The goal of this paper is to use feminist ideology to explicate how research can be a consciousness-raising experience for researchers, participants, and society. We will use examples, taken from our data on the survival of rape, to support and illustrate our methodological processes and considerations.

Our research is a response to the victims (or survivors) of one form of violence against women, rape. The feminist emphasis of our work is reflected in several critical assumptions. First, we regard our research participants as experts of their own experiences. In contrast, MacKinnon (1983) has noted that "the distance between most sexual violations of women and the legally perfect definition of rape (i.e. raped by a total stranger with witnesses) measures the imposition of someone else's definition on women's experiences" (1983: 651). Thus, if a woman's experience of sexual violation is one in which there is no proof of lack of consent on her part (beyond her own word), then her experience will not present a case easily prosecuted. The difficulty when women compare their experiences to those rapes with public validation is that they may incorporate the public view and not label their own experiences as rape. For example, one of our participants, a survivor of marital rape, had not realized that her fears and feelings about men were related to her rapes until she heard one of our community presentations. Seeing women as experts of their own experiences meant accepting women where they were in their own definitions of their experiences. More importantly, this assumption expressed itself in our work as a deep respect for women's survival skills and their own interpretation of their experiences.

The second assumption underlying our feminist beliefs is that the fundamental cause of rape is rooted in sexism in interaction with the sanctioning of violence in our society (e.g. Walker, 1979; Leidig, 1981). This perspective is at variance with the traditional psychological view of rape as a form of sexual psychopathy; as a diagnosable, treatable illness with the emphasis, therefore, on the treatment of the individual rapist's pathology. Within this perspective, not surprisingly, the raped woman has been ignored (see Carmen, Russo, & Miller, 1981; Hare-Mustin, 1983).

Finally, we assume that the cognitive and behavioral changes experienced by women following rape can be regarded as normal, positive adjustment strategies which function to reduce any deleterious effects and allow healthy psychological functioning. We do not conceive these effects as symptoms of psychopathology. Therefore, within the context of our research the raped woman has been referred to as a "survivor," rather than a "victim," of rape. The term victim is most generally used to refer to individuals who have been irreparably damaged, killed, or who are currently under attack by some deleterious force; conversely, the term "survivor" is used to refer to individuals who have lived through such an attack. The latter term with its associated images of strength/life is considered more appropriate.

From Interview to Consciousness Raising

Since we believe that the raped woman is an expert of her own experience, the methodology we have chosen is one which allows a woman to tell her story, an interview. Interview is derived from the words "entre" meaning mutually, or each other, and "voir" meaning to see: to see each other. Our structured interviews transcend the traditional interview process which has been described as an "interrogation" (Meacham, 1980). In interrogations researchers are considered experts and participants (subjects) are viewed as naive, at best. The information exchange that occurs in this process is one-sided or exploitative (Oakley, 1981), with the experimenter "demanding" information from the participants. Participants are not allowed to ask questions nor do researchers voluntarily provide them information for fear of "biasing" the responses.[1] Oakley (1981) provides an enlightened discussion of the rules that accompany the traditional interviewing process. She argues, for example, that the "contradiction between the need for 'rapport' and the requirement of between-interview comparability can not be solved" (1981: 51). Similarly, Tyler, Pargament, and Gatz (1983) have written on the paradox between presenting oneself as an expert and establishing a collaborative resource or research relationship.

Feminists have begun to articulate rules that describe a collaborative research arrangement. Oakley (1981) considered three ethical principles when defining herself as a feminist interviewer: to be non-exploitive, to provide information and feedback as requested by interviewees, and to document women's stories of their lives. The first two principles refer to the process of interviewing, and giving answers to interviewees' questions is one non-exploitive style. Consideration of the needs and privacy of those interviewed are other ways in which interviewers would minimize exploitation. Oakley's third point pertains to content and defines a style of interviewing as distinctively feminist. Although the content of women's lives can only be approached non-exploitively in order to be called feminist, non-exploitive or interactive styles have been utilized without embracing the feminist label (e.g. Meacham, 1980). Rather than "interrogation" we feel that "true" dialogue would better serve the interests of both researchers and participants by maximizing the exchange of information and subsequently, the construction of knowledge.

When the concept of a dialogue is embodied in the research interview, then participants become "co-researchers" in dialogue: the researcher and participant attempt to "see each other's" experiences and to gain from their interaction. In order to see each other, we must be open to each other's views of reality and prepare ourselves to accept that our views may differ. When we first decided to develop a structured interview to be used to investigate rape, we began the process by contacting a group of rape survivors to meet and discuss, informally, our mutual rape experiences. As we sat and listened to one another we became aware of ways of experiencing rape that were both like and unlike our own experiences. The information which accrued from these and subsequent dialogues was germane to the construction of the first draft and further revisions of our interview schedule.

The awareness of commonalities and differences in experiences can fuel a collective understanding of rape as a social rather than individual experience. This process of changing awareness through dialogue is referred to as consciousness raising, a feminist method (see MacKinnon, 1982). Traditionally, consciousness raising has been blocked by research methods that manifest a devaluation of personal experience. In regard to rape research, consciousness raising has also been impeded by the very nature of the rape experience which can be seen as isolated (in the act) and isolating in its consequences (e.g. as a target of victim blaming, cf. Ryan, 1972; Symonds, 1980; Williams & Holmes, 1981).

What has been missing in mainstream psychological and sociological research has been the reality of women's lives as women themselves define their experiences. Research is feminist when it attempts to bring forth that reality in a manner which frees women's voices from the dominant context which derives power from women's silence. Any method, even the interactive, non-hierarchical, non-exploitive, can be utilized in ways which ignore women's lives. In this time of heightened awareness of "women's issues," feminist researchers must attempt to ensure that all women's lives are voiced.

Consciousness raising is extremely important when researchers' and participants' experiences are dissimilar. Researchers can potentially distort women's realities by a failure to recognize and validate different experiences due to their own values and biases. To the extent that certain women's experiences are ignored (by virtue of racism, inaccessibility, or unpopularity of an issue, for example), then research is biased and not feminist. An example of heterosexist bias in our research was pointed out by a lesbian rape survivor. We had constructed questions on changing patterns of heterosexual dating following a rape, thereby assuming that all women who are raped are heterosexual.

The most ignored women's experiences are those which have the most radical and transformative power, because those experiences are defined by the worst aspects of our social condition (e.g. power of poverty and violence). If we only hear women's voices filtered through others who misrepresent women's experiences, we lose the transforming power of the message. In the case of research, we lose the potential of research for social change and continue a genre that disempowers women.

Researchers' lack of awareness of their own biases has also influenced the development of psychological models to describe women's responses to rape victimization (Fine, 1983). Based on their own position of privilege, researchers have concluded that individuals cope most effectively (optimally) with unjust or difficult circumstances by taking control of their environment through the utilization of available formal support systems (e.g. mental health, legal) and by assuming personal responsibility for initiating change. Fine stated that "the current taking-control arguments often assumed that people can control the forces that victimize them, should utilize available social programs, and will benefit from social supports" (1983: 3). She maintained that these universally prescribed means of coping are likely to be ineffectual for persons whose social power and privilege are limited by social class, race, gender, disability or sexual preference. Fine also maintained that for these individuals, taking control often has meant rejecting available social programs which do not meet needs and realizing that social support systems may not be reliable. According to Fine "these acts of taking control have long been neglected or misclassified by psychologists as acts of relinquishing control" (1983: 3). Furthermore, Fine noted that "as long as individual victims (survivors) act alone to improve their circumstances, oppressive economic and social arrangements will persist and be reinforced" (1983: 15).

In summary, research has the potential to affirm or negate realities, to be consciousness raising or consciousness denying. In the following sections we will explore three dialogues which may enhance consciousness raising research: (1) the researcher's internal dialogues, (2) the dialogue between researcher and participant, and (3) the dialogue between researcher and society. While these dialogues will be developed in the context of our research with the survivors of rape, the principles generalize to all social science research (cf. Meacham, 1980).

Researchers' Internal Dialogue

Consciousness raising in this domain arises from the breakdown in the distinction between private and public or subjective and objective. As women who have been raped or who live in constant fear of rape, we are both the subject and object of our research, thus obliterating distinctions between "us" and "them". This lack of differentiation, called "double consciousness" by Meis (1978), violates a prevalent social science assumption: that values (subjectivity) can be separated from research like error variance from total variance. Rather than denying the reality of our personal experiences we, as researchers, should be critical of our values and the impact of our research.

Critical awareness can be facilitated by internal dialogues in which we carefully examine our experiences and define our values and assumptions. This critical awareness can be further developed by communicating with others and evaluating their perceptions of our experiences (biases). For example, in one interview a young woman, who had been kidnapped and raped by three strangers, replied that one thing that made her angry was hearing stories from "stupid women in the dorm who get themselves in situations on dates and call this rape." Her interviewer responded with a feminist analysis of victim blaming and targeted responsibility for such "date rapes" on the perpetrator. After the interview we discussed this interchange and the way in which the interviewer's feminist bias against victim blaming may have obscured seeing the possible function served by this survivor's anger toward victims of date rape. By blaming the victim, this survivor may have been able to distance herself from her own potential vulnerability to a rape by an acquaintance she trusts. In this case, both an internal dialogue and dialogue between researchers were utilized in an attempt to overcome a bias that was working to obscure and invalidate a woman's experience.

The challenge of a feminist consciousness in research is to hold a critical awareness of the intersection of our personal experiences with those of other women. We must, for example, be wary of women's experiences which have been devalued socially (e.g. spirituality) and to whose devaluation we may contribute. The most salient example of such an experience that has been relevant in our interviews is the very privatized experience of intuition. To say that we utilize intuition and feelings in our interviews and yet not be able to specify how this is done reflects, in part, the extreme social degradation of these ways of experiencing reality. To what extent have we denied these ways of knowing to ourselves?

Participant-Researcher Dialogue

Instead of invalidating a woman's survival strategies, as exemplified above, research can operate to support a woman's experiences. This section refers to changes in consciousness in participant and researcher that accrue from the interview process. With respect to participant changes, over 90% of the women experienced their interviews as supporting and validating. They say that they have found talking about their rapes helpful and therapeutic (see also Resick, Calhoun, Atkeson, & Ellis, 1981). Many have survived their rape alone, talking about it little or not at all. Because they have attempted to survive alone, many of our participants are unaware of the effects that rape can have on women's lives. These include the occurrence of rape-related nightmares and memories, changes in levels of fear, anxiety, anger and depression, sexual dysfunction and various life restrictions (Burgess and Holmstrom, 1974, 1979a, 1979b; Ellis,

Atkeson, and Calhoun, 1981; Kilpatrick, Resick, and Vernon, 1981; Feldman-Summers, Gordon, and Meagher, 1979). Our findings on long-term survivors essentially paralleled the above but also indicated that these effects were dynamic rather then static and tended to manifest in response to specific environmental cues. The majority of raped women are able to avoid the cues through the development of various coping and adjustment strategies.

During the interview we share our research findings and our own experiences with rape. Many women enter the research process with the notion that the social and psychological changes they have continued to experience after the rape are indicative of insanity and personal inability to adjust. When a woman finds that other women, including one of the researchers, experienced similar difficulties she is extremely relieved. A particularly striking example of the above occurred during the course of an interview when a woman, raped seven years previously, stated that the rape continued to make her do "bizarre, ridiculous things." To illustrate her point the survivor related that she had recently had a flat tire on a dark, isolated road. Rather than do the "normal, sane" thing and promptly change the tire, the survivor drove to a well-lighted service station and ruined her tire rim. When the researcher responded that she and many other rape survivors would do exactly the same thing in similar circumstances, the participant expressed relief.

Another aspect of the participant-researcher dialogue is the impact that participants have on the researchers. Each of us has experienced increased sensitivity to cues related to our vulnerability to rape. Each of us has had rape-related nightmares which resulted in difficulty with sleep or sleepless nights. Subsequently, we try to limit ourselves to one interview a week. The raped woman, however, cannot so easily limit her recall nor distance herself from feelings of vulnerability. The more we interview the more we feel the impact of rape on women's lives.

Moreover, as we continue to interview, we further understand and develop respect for the diverse ways women have survived their rapes. To place our feminist survival above other ways women have coped with their experiences, as we did when we failed to realize the possible coping value of victim blaming, replicates the "researcher as expert, subject as naive" hierarchical dichotomy. Such a reproduction limits the knowledge we produce about women's experiences of rape.

Researcher-Society Dialogue

The third dialogue enhancing consciousness raising is between researcher and society. Our awareness and experience of the nature of rape is part of our social situation as researchers and is reflected in our feminist assumptions stated earlier. Perhaps the most notable social influence we contended with was our class. As a graduate student and a faculty member, we were afforded both the time and money to conduct research. Our academic situation, however, was a barrier to women who did not feel comfortable meeting with women from the university. Though we actively recruited women from lower and working class neighborhoods and offered to meet them in their homes or other place of their choice, we felt that our distance from their everyday lives was a large obstacle. Researchers who have direct knowledge of the context of women's lives are least likely to misinterpret or misrepresent the information they receive.

In order to have this direct knowledge, which approaches the role of a participant observer, researchers can not be located full-time in universities. Unfortunately, in most research the person most likely to interpret and disseminate results is the least likely to have had contact with the participants and their social context. Feminist researchers can avoid this distancing by involving themselves with people who provide supportive services to women whose lives are of research interest, or by providing those services themselves. While involved with interviewing rape survivors, we were also volunteering with our local rape crisis center, providing community training on rape-related issues, and making public presentations on the effects of rape. Such involvement both provided access to women who subsequently shared their lives with us and provided the vehicle for us to share that information with others.

Making private experiences public is the other side of a researcher-society dialectic; specifically, it is our social influence. We are particularly interested in raising the social consciousness for rape in rape survivors and others with whom they interact (e.g. families, helping agents and members of the legal profession). Moreover, rape survivors share this concern by stating they hope their experiences will help other women who have been raped.

We believe that we must utilize our privilege as researchers to go beyond the vacuum of professional dissemination qua professional advancement and bring the voices of raped women into public awareness.[2] This means deliberate attempts to introduce our research findings into arenas where access to professional literature is least likely to be available (e.g., lower class women). This can be done through popular media and community presentations. Furthermore, we introduce our research to people in social policy areas: for example, by educating judges and attorneys, as well as jurors, through expert testimony regarding rape myths (see Project Courtwatch, 1980). We are currently conducting research which shows that rape myths/facts are utilized in student, mock rape jury deliberations, and our research suggests that trial outcome is related to knowledge of rape facts (Tetreault and Bristow, 1983).

In addition, we hope to raise the consciousness of mental health workers to both the prevalence and long-term effects of rape (for example, see Koss, 1983 and Russell & Howell, 1983 on incidence and prevalence; and Emslie & Rosenfeld, 1983 on the history of incest in psychiatrically hospitalized children and adolescents). Women's "irrational" fears, sexual dysfunctions, sense of vulnerability and low self-esteem may be due to prior sexual assault(s), even ones which occurred many years ago. A woman experiencing these effects will find little or no affirmation from others that these effects are part of her rape(s). She is tempted or persuaded to create other reasons to explain her actions: for example, she may doubt her sanity. Failure to develop intervention, research and public policy that devolve from women's experiences is a failure of consciousness. In contrast, we believe that research embodying consciousness raising in its process, as articulated by feminists, is research that empowers oppressed people.

NOTES

1. In fact, the term "demand characteristics" is used to refer to those aspects of research or the researcher that create expectancies about how participants are to respond or perform and thus bias the research.

2. Tyler, Pargament and Gatz (1983) conceptualized the responsibility of unequal status as a "deprofessionalization" issue and explored some of the problems with this view (p. 392).

Research as Critical Reflection: A Study of Self, Time and Communicative Competency

Valerie Ann Malhotra

Reflexive Statement

Static, non-involved, non-dialectical forms of social science research treat the persons studied as abstract objects rather than as living persons in process. In critical reflective research, alienation from work and from product is alleviated. From an existentialist as well as a critical perspective, the research activity itself must have some value independent of the results. To me this has meant that my research design must be such that it is a justifiable activity, even if by some stroke of fate the work could never be completed. This project also realizes a long-standing desire on my part to better integrate sociological theory, research and practice.

Introduction

This paper is about research which was structured as a critically reflective process. It does not report on the substantive results of the research. Rather, its focus is on the effect of involvement in the research of those who participated. The study emphasizes the experience and use of time, the development of the self, and communicative competency among female university students. Fifty-three women students met weekly in small groups as a basis for gathering data. Multiple techniques of data collection were employed. A comparison is to be made between older (non-traditional) students and those of typical university age. A major concern of the research was on how women's lives are affected by their relative lack of power in a male-dominated order.

Theory

This research was informed by George Herbert Mead's theory of self, a phenomenological approach to the experience of time, and Habermas' concept of communicative competency. Mead's theory of self emphasizes the way in which identity depends upon the explicit and implicit attitudes and demands of others. It is therefore contrary to the concept of the autonomous individual which is prevalent in American culture. In addition, Mead emphasizes the importance of the development of reflectivity in rela- tion to personal and social change. Reflectivity to Mead does not mean merely the conscious adoption of a socially normative perspective. Rather, it makes possible a critical appraisal of cultural norms (Miller, 1973).

Mead (1959) also contributed to the awareness of the temporal basis of experience. However, a clearer insight into the importance of temporality is evident in the existential-phenomenological tradition. Heidegger (1962) bases his phenomenology of existence on temporality. Schutz (1970) did pioneer work on time as experienced in contrast to objective, external time. This theoretical work makes it evident that knowledge of the experiential aspects of time may be critical to the understanding of any person (see Guajardo, 1980). Emancipation, if it occurs, will show its hand in an opening up of the experience of time and in changes in its actual use.

Habermas' insights into the pervasion of strategic communication and power-distorted communication are particularly relevant in relation to women. Habermas delineates four validity claims which underlie all attempts at communication motivated to achieve understanding. The four validity claims are: comprehensibility (statements make sense), objective truth (statements represent actual states of affairs), truthfulness (statements are not intended to deceive), and rightness (statements are normatively appropriate). The groups were guided to facilitate a communications and data-gathering process in which these claims of competent communication could be met.

Methodology

It is important that research about oppressed groups attempts to alleviate repressive and exploitative aspects of the research process itself. Oppressed and vulnerable persons such as minorities, mental patients, the elderly, and students are frequently the objects of social research. Typically, such research is structured to reinforce an alienated relationship between "researcher" and "subject." That is, oppressed groups are involved in relationships with others which benefit those in power to a greater extent than the oppressed group benefits. In traditional research, the subjects typically provide information over which they have no control, both in terms of how it is obtained and how it is used. Beneficiaries of the research are usually those who sponsor the research and those who get credit for its accomplishment.

Steps are taken in the structuring of this project to alleviate these effects. To begin, the providers of narratives and documents were called "participants" rather than "subjects." This symbolizes a shift away from the asymmetrical researcher/subject tradition. In addition, participants were involved in small group discussions through which they had an impact on the methodologies. These groups also functioned as support-growth groups.

Participants had the option of choosing not to provide any aspect of the data. This option was used. One woman did not produce the audiotape of a dinner conversation at home due to a custody battle with her former husband over her teen-age daughter. This daughter had refused to be taped. If participants chose to provide data, they were under no pressure to disclose information that they preferred to keep to themselves. It is evident in the narrative texts provided by participants that the depth of their involvement in the process varied. Some diaries are soliloquies about deeply personal and important conflicts. Although she said little in the group discussions, one woman used her diary to explore her feelings about her disintegrating marriage:

> Only the second day into my journal, and I have to write that my husband wants to leave me. Why don't I feel devastated? But I do. All I can think of is that we finally talked!
> The weekends are the hardest to bear. I stay quite busy, allowing little time to think about my

circumstances. Today is typical. I shopped and cleaned and cooked. My husband left about six. He said he didn't know if he would come back tonight. I knew he wouldn't. I don't ask where he is going. The older two kids go out for the evening. The youngest has a friend over to stay the night. If he gets a good report from the counselor, he can go out next weekend. I sip a glass of wine and study. It's lonely though.

In contrast to this example, some diaries were written at a superficial level. Therefore pressures upon participants in regard to level of disclosure were minimal. The depth of self-reflection was at each woman's discretion.

In addition, participants were encouraged to be involved at all levels of the research process including involvement in data analysis, writing and presenting results. Two participants were later employed as data coders. Four participants wrote and presented professional papers about the research, and several have assisted in coding and data analysis. One participant intends to write her dissertation using aspects of the data.

The norms surrounding the functioning of small groups facilitated communicative competency in Habermas' sense. Confidentiality was a working agreement in the groups. Anonymity of the documents was guaranteed by signed agreement with the researcher. In order for speech acts to qualify as "undistorted," attempts must be made to allow for the actualization of the validity claims of comprehensibility, truth, truthfulness, and normative appropriateness. Since the discussions were unrestricted, institutionally based value judgements were not imposed upon the discussions. Thus, it was less likely that strategic action, or action governed by institutional demands, would distort understanding. Also, the discussions were about everyday life experiences, but they took place out of their usual context. Such context-independent discussions free acts from immediate consequences, thus making them less vulnerable to self-imposed distortions based on fears.

In addition, the self-reflective processes involved were similar in some ways to a psychoanalytic hermeneutic process. The small groups provided the occasion for a critical eye to be cast upon childhood and cultural influences upon the self. The effect of early primary relationships on current patterns of activities was a focus of both the autobiographical and the phenomenological time studies and the discussions surrounding them. Of course, we cannot know to what extent even the most intimate disclosures were absolutely truthful. However, we observed changes in behaviors such as increased expressiveness. It is also possible to check the truth content of claims by comparing one set of documents with another, or by comparing statements made in discussions with the written narratives.

Marilyn French's novel <u>The Women's Room</u> was read and discussed at initial group meetings to facilitate reflection about their situation as female students. This is a novel about women's confrontations with male domination in their personal lives and, particularly, in work and education. In this way, participants could openly discuss their feelings about issues without having to talk directly and immediately about themselves. Blockages to critical reflection were evident. For example, participants who reported experiences very much like those of the more victimized characters in the novel often condemned it. Their condemnation took several forms. One participant commented on the accuracy of the novel's descriptions of the experiences of women and gave examples from her own life of similar experiences. She did not like the novel, however, because she found it "depressing" to think about these things.

Several others displayed a hostile attitude toward the novel and were silent as to whether or not they had similar experiences. Their autobiographies and diaries indicate, however, that they did have similar experiences. One woman wrote that she "struggled through most of it and then had to quit" because she was dealing with similar problems in her own life. Another wrote that it made her depressed; she could not discuss it in the group; "I never wanted no (sic) one to know that much about this part of my life."

Data Collection

The data collection process and the group sessions took place over a thirteen week period between September 1981 and May 1982. Each of the data collection techniques was designed to involve the participants in a self-reflective process geared towards greater critical self-awareness and towards awareness of the grounding of each individual existence in particular social-historical circumstances. The self-reflection involved in the data collection process occurred simultaneously with the participants' involvement in weekly three-hour small group discussions. These groups stimulated critical analysis and provided support. Each group was videotaped both early and late in the term. Through observation and preliminary review of the documents, it is evident that the women formed a trusting, close relationship. During these weekly sessions, the feelings, concerns and events which participants thought important were discussed. These sessions also helped them remember significant events.

Multiple data collection techniques were used throughout the project. Each participant completed a time schedule indicating how she spent the week before the term started, with whom she spent time, and her feelings about each activity. Three additional weekly time schedules were completed at monthly intervals to provide a comparison. Next, an autobiography was written by each woman, stressing perceived attributions and expectations of significant others, groups, and society at various stages of life (see Malhotra, 1977).

Reflective time series (phenomenological time studies) were then completed for three stages: when in the first grade, when first married or at age twenty-one, and today. Next, each participant tape-recorded, transcribed and analyzed a dinner-table conversation in her home in order to study direct interaction with significant others along with the effect of power on communication. Throughout the process, participants kept daily journals (diaries) to provide them with an opportunity to record and analyze relevant experiences. As a result of this intensive data collection, over one-hundred pages of richly qualitative data exists for each of the participants.

Effects of Research on Participants

Each major aspect of the research was evaluated in terms of its effect on the participants. They were asked if that aspect, such as the writing of autobiographies, had changed any of their understandings of themselves or others, and if so, how. In addition, they were asked to what extent, if any, participation in the research had changed the way they actually acted in relation to others. This paper presents an analysis of responses in the context of the observations of the researcher, who also served as facilitator in two of the four research groups.

Conversational Analysis

Participants tape-recorded and transcribed one hour of normal dinner-time conversation between themselves and family members. If they were not living with family they recorded themselves with close friends. They were asked to analyze the conversation in terms of power relationships evident in the control and content of conversations. The technique of conversational analysis employed was inspired by Habermas' concern with the distortive effects of power on communication. Ethnomethodological techniques of analysis of such factors as turn-taking, interruptions, paired utterances, glossings, and the search for normal forms were utilized (Cicourel, 1963; Speier, 1973). This technique of data collection and analysis has been previously tested (Malhotra and Deneen, 1982).

Twenty-six percent (n = 14) of the participants did not complete this aspect of the research because of fears on their part or on the part of family members. Indeed, the conversational analysis was the most intrusive of the techniques used.

Thirty-two percent (n = 17) of participants reported having changed their behavior as well as understanding as a result of doing the conversational analysis. Some of the behavioral changes indicated were the following: showing more respect and appreciation for family members, turning off the television more frequently, being either more or less assertive in conversation, becoming more humorous and less critical, becoming less defensive in interaction with a domineering husband, and becoming more fair with children.

Thirty percent (n = 16) reported changed understandings only. Increased awareness of the following were reported: multiple interpretations of situations, poor usage of language, the influence of self on others, and the need to become more self confident. Twelve percent (n = 6) reported no effect from having completed the conversational analysis.

Daily Journals

The daily journals kept by the women were doubly reflective, for in them they wrote about their experiences in the research, as well as other aspects of their lives at home and as students. In one of the journals a participant indicated that after a group session her husband had asked her what they had talked about. After she told him it was about the double burden of student-wives at home and at school, her husband voluntarily cooked lunch and dinner for the first time in their five-year marriage!

Participants reporting on the effects of writing and discussing the journals varied in their responses. Forty-two percent (n = 23) reported a change in understanding as a result of keeping the daily journal. One participant realized that she became too upset about some things. Some learned about the causes of their behavior; most realized that their problems were not unique but experienced by others. In Mills' (1959) sense they were able to convert their troubles into issues.

A great variety of behavioral changes were reported by forty percent (n = 21) of the participants resulting from writing in their daily journals. Changes in family interactions included the following: becoming more distant from husband, starting to yell at husband, a change in sex life, becoming more assertive, and putting less pressure on husband and children. Other reported changes included: becoming a "new self," becoming more patient, learning to say "no," making better use of time, improving personality traits, and learning to set priorities. Eighteen percent (n = 10) reported no effects.

For some participants, it was difficult to say whether they should be attributed with a change in understanding or in behavior. For them, the act of writing the journal was in itself a behavior with certain direct effects. These were: release of hostility, the experience of pain in writing, and feeling better while writing. The journals' value was described by one participant, who was also a research assistant, as "therapeutic." She indicated that the journals showed how the various aspects of the research, the self, temporality, and communicative competency were integrated (Stable, 1981). She described the therapeutic advantages of the journals for the women as including the following: monitoring one's own behavior and environmental influences, exploring the possibilities and limitations of one's own life space, working out role conflicts, providing support for self-nurturance, being able to see oneself more positively, and clarifying goals. Commenting on this aspect of the journals, Stabel said:

> In suggesting the use of a journal for therapeutic as well as research purposes, we do not in any way encourage it as an end in itself, or as a substitute for action. However, it can serve as a kind of blueprint in which to chart new and desirable courses of action.

The therapeutic effect may not only go hand in hand with critical practice, but may be a necessary motivation for it.

Time Schedules

The self is temporally expressed through activities and role enactments. Participants reflected on the keeping of four weekly time schedules. Forty-two percent (n = 23) of the participants reported that having kept and discussed the time schedules had changed their understandings. They reported greater awareness of the following: their use of time, of their subservience to the demands of others, their own selfishness with time, their frustrations and feelings surrounding time use. They also reported increased appreciation for how much they do.

Thirty-two percent (n = 17) reported not only a change in understanding, but a change in behavior as well. Many of them adjusted their use of time to better reflect their goals and values. Family patterns of responsibility were changed in some cases. Decisions were made to be more lax about housework or to obtain help from family members. Twenty-one percent (n = 11) reported no effect of the time schedules.

A participant who gave a presentation on the effect of keeping and discussing the time schedules used the phrase "making nothing a reality" to describe the results of this reflective exercise (Owens, 1981). She had spoken with other participants about the effects of keeping the time schedules. They reported realizing how much they did even though they would respond "nothing" if asked what they had done on a given day. This was especially true of the married students and student mothers. The time schedules kept the week prior to entering school showed the women assisting children and spouses in preparing for school and work activities, with no time to prepare themselves, and no one assisting them in their preparations.

Autobiographies

Systematic reflection on childhood influences and influences of parents and additional significant others was a new experience for all participants. The discussions surrounding this process were frequently highly emotional. Several women discussed early experiences involving severe physical and verbal abusiveness on the part of parents or spouses. They received understanding and support from the group.

Fifty-one percent (n = 27) of the participants reported that writing the autobiography had changed their understandings. They reported such effects as more awareness of the following: the effects of others on them, the causes of their own behavior, their own past, their own limitations, their own role in making life choices, and the effect they had on others. Some reported having greater acceptance of their own lives and greater acceptance of others. One said her childhood goals were reinforced through participation.

Thirty-seven percent (n = 20) of the participants reported changes in behavior resulting from writing and discussing the autobiographies. Among these changes were: greater strictness with children, less tolerance of others' lack of responsibility, developing the motivation to begin a new project, greater self-confidence, improved relationships with significant others, and entering psychotherapy.

Phenomenological Time Studies

Participants were trained to use serial sensory bracketing in phenomenological studies of experience at three points in time: first grade, at age twenty-one or when first married, and the present. Participants were asked to recall the events of a day in terms of sensory memories--one at a time. Things seen, heard, smelled and touched throughout the day at each point in time were to be recalled, along with any significant feelings, events and other persons involved in the recollected experience.

In the group discussions, it was evident that emotionally significant contents were emerging from the exercise. Fifty-seven percent (n = 30) reported changed understandings as a result of doing and discussing the phenomenological time studies. They reported such effects as greater acceptance of others, greater sensory awareness, and realization of the bases of their morals and values in their own past.

Those reporting a changed behavior from this aspect of the project totaled thirty percent (n = 16). They reported the following changes: different reactions from others, a tendency to look more towards the present rather than to the future, making more of their own decisions, gaining greater acceptance of their own pasts, changing their perceptions of things and events, and entering psychotherapy. Four percent (n = 2) reported no effect from having completed the phenomenological time studies.

Conclusions

This research was designed to increase the self-reflective awareness of the participants as they wrote self-descriptive and analytical narratives. The small discussion groups were structured to facilitate communication freed from power or distortions based on strategic interests. In this way, the relatively undistorted communication in the groups stimulated the private recollective and reflective activities of the women. Extensive validation of the effects of the process can only be accomplished as the data are analyzed. However, initial reading of the documents, in addition to the participants' reports on the effects of involvement in the research, indicated that the reflective activities caused changes in their understandings and behaviors. Table 1 summarizes these reported effects:

TABLE 1
Reported Effects of Five Research Techniques on Participants

Effect	N	Percent
Changed Behavior and Understandings	18	34
Changed Understandings Only	24	45
No Effect Reported	6	12
Not Completed	5	9
Total	53	100

Habermas' critical theory of communication oriented towards understanding, Mead's theory of self and the reflective process, and Schutz' emphasis on the importance of the experience of time, provided the theoretical and methodological bases for this study. Yet even the power and insight of these theories and methods inevitably fall short of the subject. The richness and depth of the lives of the women involved in the study are only dimly captured in the documents. At least some appreciation of the heroic efforts of women students who function in several worlds in positions of relative powerlessness was gained.

In spite of the changes expressed, the reflective processes begun in the research must be seen as incomplete and fragmented beginnings. In the short period of time (fifteen weeks) in which the groups met and the research was carried out, attention was focused on those aspects of their situations which were most immediately troublesome. Underneath the discussions and reflections were the social and economic structures which define everything human, animal, vegetable or mineral as an object to be utilized for the production of profit. Even were women to attain social and economic equality with men, they would still find vast areas of shared oppressions. One of these common oppressions is the apparatus of social scientific research, which by its predominate methodologies increases the alienation of its objects at the same time that it tends to facilitate the maintenance of power. It is hoped that this project is a small example of how research may de-alienate by facilitating critical reflection.

ACKNOWLEDGEMENTS

I am grateful for the assistance of the following to the aspects of the research presented in this paper: Carole Stabel, Jerrian Stem, Tamera Bryant, Jeffrey LaMar Deneen, Dai-Na Sun, Peggy Maher and Shirley Rombough. Beth Germscheid helped with typing and editing. The women who participated in the project by providing documents and by being involved in the study groups made the study possible. They gave freely and generously of their time and of themselves.

Consideration of Ethical Issues in the Assessment of Feminist Projects: A Case Study Using Illuminative Evaluation

Joan Poliner Shapiro and *Beth Reed*

Introduction

There are considerable problems inherent in evaluating feminist projects. The approach used must address both the innovative, interdisciplinary nature of these programs and their long-range implications; we must also address ethical issues associated with these projects. In most cases, those who evaluate such programs utilize conventional measuring instruments. The advantage of using these instruments is that they are tried and tested and acceptable to the "gatekeepers" in the field of evaluation. This begs the questions: Tried and tested on what? Acceptable to whom?

Have these instruments been tested only on traditional projects within the Academy? Can these instruments really assess the very special non-traditional nature of feminist projects? Do these instruments, whether they be attitudinal surveys, developmental stage measures, pre- and post-tests, determine the subtle and not-so-subtle goals of the designers of these projects? Do the psychological measurement instruments assess the participatory interactions between the personnel and participants of these projects? Do they measure the intended and unintended consequences of an innovative proposal? Do they take into account the long-range implications of a new project? Are the measures sufficiently eclectic to assess all that the project director hopes to accomplish? Do these evaluative instruments transcend the disciplines, not only providing traditional data collection and analysis but also enabling diverse information to be valued and counted? Are the approaches utilized appropriate to the intent of many of these projects to break down the barriers between the disciplines and to challenge the traditional curriculum in universities and colleges? Above all, are these techniques and approaches compatible with feminist theory, methodology and ethics?

The above questions are the major ones which need to be considered in determining the kind of evaluative methodology to be used to select feminist projects. Numerous feminist critics of traditional evaluative approaches have asked similar questions and have raised some ethical issues in an attempt to choose the best method for assessing these projects.

Traditional Evaluation: Ethical Issues Raised by Feminist Critics

Feminist scholars have criticized an implicit axiom in research and evaluation "that the choice of a problem is determined by method instead of a method being determined by the problem" (Daly, 1978). In particular, when this unstated but traditional emphasis on the method, rather than on the program or subjects being studied, has been applied to feminist projects, the investigations have ended up being on women and not for women (Duelli-Klein, 1980). Indeed, the accepted, male-dominated view of research and evaluation has led Westkott (1979) and Eichler (1981) to find fault with traditional investigations because of the types of questions asked, the techniques used, and the conclusions drawn. The masculine model is further criticized by the Nebraska Sociological Feminist Collective (1983) when its members question the continued use of a patriarchal world view applied to feminist subjects. To them, there is a need for a feminist ethic which recognizes the oppression of women in research, work and social structures through the traditional and constant utilization of a patriarchal theory and practice in the social sciences. The Collective expresses dissatisfaction with the continued use of women as research objects. Harding and Hintikka (1983) also present an effective critical appraisal of the "distinctively masculine perspectives on masculine experience" and identify in their book "distinctive aspects of women's experience which can provide resources for the construction of more representatively human understanding" (1983: p. x). Stanley and Wise's (1983) critique indicates the need for a "feminist social science" where personal and direct experiences are recognized. Criticisms of this nature emphasize the very real importance of developing new or modifying old methodologies, especially, but not only, for studies of feminist projects.

Beyond raising ethical questions about evaluative methodologies, feminists have criticized the traditional object/subject split between "the evaluator" and "those being assessed." Duelli-Klein doubts whether the detached and neutral outside evaluator is acceptable to those involved in feminist projects, since their settings are usually highly participatory and democratic. Oakley (1981) too raises objections to the one-way process in traditional interviewing and the need to be uninvolved. She writes about a two-way dialogue between interviewer and interviewee and believes it is the way for theory and practice to meld to elicit personal responses to women's experiences. In predominately female settings, personal responses, as well as factual knowledge, are often discussed and valued. The traditional remoteness and lack of involvement of the evaluator may be in conflict with the high level of commitment and the willingness to share personal experiences of those participating in the project. In addition, the removed, "objective" evaluator, who lacks understanding and sympathy for the social-change goals inherent in any feminist project, is likely to carry an unintentional bias into the evaluation. Passivity and neutrality can hinder the development of rapport between the researcher and those in the program being studied. In fact, most feminists do not expect an evaluator to approach a new project free of preconceived ideas. They do not expect the total absence of perspective and bias, which is an underlying assumption of most traditional methodologies. Instead, they welcome explicit acknowledgement of points of view. Some use the term "conscious subjectivity" (Coyner, 1980) to name a process which permits different perspectives to be presented and acknowledges that evaluators also may speak.

Illuminative Evaluation

In 1969, Malcolm Parlet introduced the approach known as illuminative evaluation in a Massachusetts Institute of Technology research study on undergraduate teaching. The concept was further developed by Trow (1970) in a paper entitled, "Methodological Problems in the Evaluation of Innovation." Since that time, this type of evaluation has gained followers both in the U.S. and in the U.K.

Illuminative evaluation is not part of the experimental and psychometric tradition. It is much more a part of the anthropological research paradigm. However, it goes beyond the anthropological approach, utilizing not only observation, interviews and documents for background information but incorporating questionnaires and other quantifiable measures where appropriate. In this way, both qualitative and quantitative methods combine to illuminate the subject.

As defined by Parlet and Hamilton (1978), "illuminative evaluation is not a standard methodological package but a general strategy. It aims to be both adaptable and eclectic. The choice of research tactics follows not from research doctrine, but from decisions in each case as to the best available techniques; the problem defines the methods, not *vice versa*" (1978: 13).

An important aspect of illuminative evaluation is that it neither claims to be value free nor to be capable of total objectivity. It does try to represent diverse beliefs, ideologies, and opinions that may be encountered in the course of the study, and to represent differences of thought and perspectives in ways considered fair by those holding the views. This fairness is often negotiated by sharing collected and analyzed data with those involved in the assessment process as frequently as possible for their comments; and it is achieved by a willingness on the part of the evaluator to dismiss data which are thought to be particularly biased and unfairly interpreted by the assessor. Another part of the illuminative model is the acknowledgment of the duality of the evaluator's role as both knowledgeable insider and, at the same time, independent outsider. Also, a purpose of illuminative evaluation is intervention; it attempts to promote changes in the way people view educational processes (Parlet & Dearden, 1977). Because of this emphasis on change, illuminative evaluation has been recommended for the assessment of innovative programs (Shapiro, Secor & Butchart, 1983). Additionally, its varied techniques can provide both program planners and funding agencies with the kinds of quantifiable data they often require. Finally, it can offer a picture which includes the often subtle qualities without which our understanding of the program would be incomplete and possibly skewed.

In theory, illuminative evaluation seemed especially appropriate as a way to assess the strengths and weaknesses of the first National Summer Institute in Women's Studies, while it also provided a qualitative sense of the Institute's dynamics and shape. In line with such feminist thinking, the illuminative evaluation process focused less on pre-determined methodologies and more on the use of techniques appropriate to participant and staff interactions: participants could be involved in the assessment process; there was no claim of perfect objectivity; and the evaluation consultant was expected to function as a participant-observer rather than as a distant, impartial outsider. Therefore, illuminative evaluation seemed to have special merits and to be compatible with both staff and participants' need for involvement with the evaluation process. In practice, this mode of evaluation worked well. Following is a description of the adaptation of illuminative evaluation in meeting the special needs of program developers, staff, and participants.

The Statement of the Problem

The context for this study was a three-week Institute which involved the two authors of this chapter, one as an evaluative consultant and the other as director. Because this was a new experimental venture, the atmosphere was charged with excitement, and the evaluation was also therefore deemed of unusual importance by both staff and participants. One major concern was for compatibility of the assessment approach with feminist theoretical and ethical perspectives. Also, the desire to be involved in the evaluative process, typical of feminist groups, was probably heightened in this particular context. The Institute therefore provided an unusually challenging test of illuminative evaluation.

Two questions formed the basis of this chapter:

1) "To what extent can and should the evaluator maintain an independent and objective role within a feminist project, given the theoretical perspectives of those involved and the intense intellectual, personal, and political involvement that such a project generates?" and,

2) "In what ways and why is illuminative evaluation a suitable methodology for assessing feminist projects?"

Description of the Feminist Institute

A three-week National Summer Institute in Women's Studies, the first of its kind in the country, was launched in 1981 by the Great Lakes Colleges Association. Entitled, "Towards a Feminist Transformation of the Curriculum" and planned as an annual event, the Institute was substantially supported in its first two years by a grant from the Lilly Endowment. It was designed to provide faculty and administrators (up to forty-eight participants per summer), already experienced in Women's Studies at the higher education level, with an opportunity to combine an intensive exploration of feminist theory with an examination of practical issues related to teaching and curriculum development. Each applicant was asked to state how the experience "can contribute to your ability as a feminist, to affect educational change" and to describe a project to be pursued during the Institute, for implementation on her or his campus during the year following the Institute (projects including the development of a new Women's Studies course, the transformation of an existinig course within a department, the design of a faculty development project in Women's Studies, etc.). The major goal of the Institute was to provide a group of committed feminists with rich resources and a community of dialogue and support that would help them become more effective catalysts for curricular change within their institutions.

The Institute brought together forty-five participants from all regions of the U.S., and four participants from Great Britain, Switzerland and the Netherlands. Ninety-six per cent of the participants were women. Fifty per cent were 31-40 years of age, and 29 per cent were 41-50 years old. Nearly 75 per cent of those involved received 100 per cent financial support from their institutions to attend. They came from state universities, community colleges, private women's and co-educational liberal arts colleges. Over 35 per cent of the participants were assistant professors or associate professors. When questioned, 70 per cent considered their major responsibility to be teaching, although many of them were also involved in Women's Studies or other areas of academic administration.

In addition to the director and assistant director, there were thirteen staff members, representing a range of disciplines, teaching, and administrative experience. While the participant group lacked racial or ethnic diversity, the staff included two Black women from the U.S. and a Chilean teaching in this country. The staff determined in advance that the Institute would focus on the following critical issues: sex discrimination, racism, class bias, and the implications of institutionalized heterosexuality. The decision emerged from the staff's own effort to come to grips with these personal and political issues. The critical issues were debated and continually explored throughout the Institute. Although never completely resolved, the discussion of these issues enabled both the staff and participants to challenge traditional assumptions of the academy.

Colleges and universities, which traditionally have almost totally omitted the study of women's lives and experiences in their curricula, administrative policies and procedures, have only painfully and slowly begun to change. The work of challenging the disciplines and changing the curriculum has barely begun. Yet working toward creating an inclusive academy, not focused merely on privileged white males, is highly exciting, and involves asking new questions about the structure of knowledge and the purposes of higher education. Today, this work is enjoying the interest of an increasing number of men as well as women. The commitment of participants in an Institute of this kind was therefore certain to be intense, since feminist theoretical perspectives and their application were upper-most in people's minds. Thus, most individuals were concerned not only with their own participation in the Institute, but with the assessment process itself. In this highly critical environment, many asked either directly or indirectly: <u>Who would evaluate this intensive experience, how would it be done, and what would happen with the data collected during the Institute?</u>

In this intellectually stimulating setting, all of the traditional assessment processes and procedures derived from the social sciences were challenged and discussed. Neutrality and objectivity in evaluation were argued against. Bias was thought to be inevitable and potentially useful, if made explicit. Involvement at all stages of the assessment process by Institute participants, staff, and administrators was desired and requested.

Description of the Evaluation

Evaluation Consultant

From the outset, the director of the Institute envisioned the evaluation of the project as a collaborative process. Even in the proposal requesting funds for the Institute, she spoke of appointing an "evaluation consultant," not an "evaluator." In her mind, a person sympathetic to the project would be most useful, and no outside, impartial observer was considered. Instead, collegiality was sought. Although continuous collaboration throughout the evaluation was never discussed, it was evident to the evaluation consultant that some type of collaborative venture was intended.

A model for illuminative evaluation, consisting of a combination of qualitative and quantitative techniques, was designed. Quantifiable information was obtained both through a needs assessment form, filled out by participants and staff early in the Institute, and through specific questions on the evaluation form. Qualitative information was obtained through observations of the formal and informal sessions and staff meetings, and through open-ended questions on the evaluation form. The evaluation consultant was on-site for an eight-day period: four days at the beginning of the Institute and four at the end. She also kept in close telephone contact with the program director.

Although both the evaluation consultant and the Institute director recognized that feminists might want to take part in the evaluation process, the extent to which involvement was sought came as a surprise to them. From the very outset, the director, advisor, staff, and participants indicated that they wished to be a part of every aspect of the assessment process, from the formulation of questions, to the staff's preparation of materials they wished to have included in the final report. Many of the requests for collaboration were granted.

An example of this type of intensive involvement can be seen in the development of the final questionnaire for participants. Towards the end of the Institute, the evaluation consultant designed an assessment instrument. She then showed the form to the director and advisor of the project, and together they made significant revisions in both the language and content of the questionnaire. Subsequently, the director and advisor asked that all staff review the instrument. Each staff member proposed changes; and two of the teaching staff also shared the questionnaire with their workshop participants, who suggested further revisions. The evaluation consultant analyzed and synthesized these suggestions and modified the original instrument markedly. Only one hour prior to its distribution was the questionnaire completed!

Evaluation Process

Below are summarized some interactions which occurred between the evaluation consultant and the director, advisor, staff, and participants during and immediately after the Institute:

1. Between evaluation consultant and program planners. The director and advisor communicated with the

evaluator throughout the evaluation process; they helped to develop the needs assessment form and refined the questionnaire; they assisted in the selection of staff to be interviewed; they indicated the importance of staff and participant involvement in the assessment process; and they designed and organized the sessions in which the staff would give their final evaluations.

2. Between the evaluation consultant and the staff. The evaluator observed representative staff members in their theory and teaching seminars; representative staff were interviewed in an unstructured format; representative individuals were asked to contribute to the formulation of items for the final questionnaire before it was distributed; all staff met in small groups at the conclusion of the Institute to evaluate both the structure and the process and to make recommendations for future Institutes (the staff then met as a whole for reporting and synthesizing data from the small groups); and all staff members made recommendations for future Institutes.

3. Between the evaluation consultant and the participants. Participants selected on the basis of their race, class, age, sex, and years of experience in the field of Women's Studies, were observed in seminar and workshop sessions and interviewed in an unstructured format; other participants, who wished to be interviewed but were not chosen as representative of a particular variable were able to be part of the process; and a few participants critiqued the evaluation form and suggested changes (some of which were made, others not).

Presentation of the Data

In this collaborative setting, preparation of the final report of the Institute posed two major problems: 1. For whom was it intended? and 2. How should it be used? From the outset of the project, the director of the Institute wanted evaluative data for three purposes, which are listed here according to priority. First of all, she requested qualitative and quantitative data to use toward revising the Institute in its second year. Next, she wanted to provide information needed by the sponsoring association and by the foundation contributing financial support to the Institute. Finally, she thought it important to document this experience for historical purposes.

Taking these needs into account, the evaluation consultant focused a great deal of attention on information collected for the purposes of strengthening and improving the design of "Year Two" of the Institute. She also attempted to synthesize enough data to satisfy the requirements of the president of the director's organization and the foundation officer, and to provide a written record of the First National Women's Studies Institute.

Data were presented in diverse ways in the final report. Participant profiles were all reported as percentages. Satisfaction indices were designated using percentages, while comments by staff and participants were displayed in a narrative fashion. To assist the director and funding agency in making judgments, comments were consolidated and the number of participants responding in a similar way was indicated in the right-hand margin. For example, the qualitative data were presented as Table 1:

TABLE 1

Sources of Funding to Attend Institute

Major Comments   # of Participants

Obtained support through faculty development fund   (3)

Minor Comments:

Applied for a scholarship   (1)
Obtained student funds awarded by ethnic student-
  faculty committee   (1)
Supported by fund at the college for Institute
  participants   (1)

Discussion of the Results and Conclusion

In this highly participatory environment in which the focus was on feminist issues, the evaluation consultant learned that total neutrality and objectivity were neither expected nor desired by those involved in the project. During the Institute, the evaluator had to make decisions which resulted in her becoming more of a participant and less of an observer, for she was gaining knowledge which could help change the dynamics of the Institute as it was happening.

The involved procedure of designing the final questionnaire was one indication of the collaboration which was expected from her. Although the process of conferring with Institute personnel and participants was time-consuming and taxing for the evaluation consultant, the questionnaire was much clearer and more inclusive because of it. Further, many felt directly involved in the evaluation procedure. The evaluation consultant noted that an unusually small number of complaints were made to her and to the director, concerning the questionnaire itself, and that some participants specifically expressed positive comments about it. She also noted that a few individuals whose comments had not been solicited in the early stages of revising the instrument expressed dislike of the questionnaire. Involvement or lack thereof apparently made a difference in reactions for or against the instrument.

From an evaluative standpoint, what does such criticism mean? Feminist researchers Westkott (1979) and Eichler (1980) point out that feminist criticism of traditional studies focuses on the questions asked, the techniques used, and the conclusions drawn. In this project, although not traditional, reactions were indeed of this nature. Nevertheless, when there had been sufficient opportunity for criticism and suggestions prior to the completion of the questionnaire, the final instrument was much improved and the attitude of participants, while completing the form, was very positive. Thus, it could be concluded that a stance of independence and objectivity by the evaluator would, in this feminist setting, have been detrimental to the assessment process and would not have met the particular needs of Institute staff and participants.

Illuminative evaluation empowered the program developers, staff and participants alike. It enabled all of their voices to be heard not only in the final report but throughout the Institute. All of the groups clearly indicated their likes and dislikes of the Institute and of the evaluation process itself. Through involvement in the process of deciding whom to interview and how to phrase a question, participants could speak of their own lives and experiences. They could also answer questions on a questionnaire that were jargon-free and site-specific.

In addition, the findings of this study indicate that illuminative evaluation shows promise as one evaluation methodology compatible with feminist activity and theoretical concerns. In line with the purposes of the evaluation which the director of the Institute had in mind, the illuminative evaluation model enabled preparation of a report that could offer both qualitative and quantitative data useful in designing the next year's Institute. It could also provide information that would help ensure continued funding of the project and include documentation of the first year of the Institute both as an historical record and as a chronicle for staff and past participants. As the report was very large, and funds were very low, staff received a substantial part, but not all, of the report, and participants were invited to read portions of the document in the Great Lakes Colleges Association office.

Epilogue

At the request of the director, the second Summer Institute was evaluated using illuminative evaluation.

Prior to the first sessions, the evaluator introduced the illuminative evaluation process once again to the director, the staff (three-quarters old and one-quarter new), and the new participants. Learning from the previous year's experiences, the evaluator was prepared for and invited revision of the questionnaire and the evaluative process itself by program planners, staff and participants.

Indeed modifications and changes did take place. The questionnaire was revised five times until the recommendations for changes were accepted by all of the staff. Additionally, beyond an interest in the questionnaire, there was increased emphasis on the need to interview in-depth all of the institute staff. The interviewing process became very important and much time was allotted to this procedure. This change in evaluation emphasis was an interesting development; it proably reflected the decreased needs of the funding agency and the more subtle demands of the Summer Institute personnel. Not locked into place by a fixed protocol, the procedure that comprised the illuminative evaluation process could be adjusted to meet the new demands of personnel and participants in the Institute.

Since completion of the Summer Institute, illuminative evaluation has been used to assess a number of different workshops, meetings and conferences. It was utilized very effectively in the evaluation of Wheaton College's integration project to transform the institution's total curriculum with the new scholarship on women. In fact, Tolpin (1984), the evaluator of the Wheaton experiment, called the finished assessment process, "Wheaton's illuminative evaluation of itself".

ACKNOWLEDGMENTS

The authors acknowledge with gratitude support for this study from the Lilly Endowment. Aspects of this paper were presented at the American Educational Research Association Annual Meeting, March 19-23, 1982, in New York City, New York.

Prescribed Passivity: The Language of Sexism

Julia Penelope

The recent controversy concerning the use and reference of so-called "generics" in the English language reveals the extent, if not the nature, of the political investment at stake in preserving the myth of generalized reference. Before I offer my data and observations regarding this myth, I would like to emphasize that the arguments supporting generics, especially m<u>a</u>n, m<u>e</u>n, and mank<u>ind</u>, are not substantive, but political, and those who would like to maintain the use of masculine nouns as general references are relying on popular misconceptions, n<u>ot</u> linguistic data. Of course, if linguistic history provides clues to the outcome of this controversy, I have to conclude that popular misconceptions (those definitions with the most political power backing them) will prevail, and the data I present here will become another set of "interesting" historical articles that we will choose to ignore because the evidence is embarrassing. On the basis of my evidence, there are no "generics" in English. I have found that that portion of our vocabulary that refers to human beings is divided into two unequal sub-classes, wom<u>a</u>n and m<u>a</u>n. By far, the larger sub-class contains those nouns that designate the affairs of men.

----
*   This article first appeared in Reza Ordonbadian and Walburga Von-Raffler Engel, <u>Views on Language</u> (1975); Murfreesboro, Tenn: Inter-University Publishing. Pp. 96-108.

As others have observed, men have been the doers and the actors, the central figures in their histories, and those nouns that refer to traditionally prestigious social positions and occupations carry (+male) as an inherent semantic feature, e.g., <u>doctor</u>, <u>lawyer</u>, <u>judge</u>, <u>chairman</u>. Only a few nouns carry the inherent feature (+female) (or -male as Geoffrey Leech would mark them), e.g., <u>nurse</u>, <u>prostitute</u>, <u>secretary</u>, <u>spider</u>, <u>housewife</u>. As a consequence, when women take up activities outside their roles as wife and/or mother, we move into <u>negative semantic space</u>, semantic space that does not exist for us. When a woman occupies a professional position usually reserved for men, she does not move into the semantic space covered by the "standard" occupational label. Instead, her anomalous position must be marked by the addition of a special "female marker"; we insert <u>woman/female/lady</u> in front of the occupational term, e.g., <u>lady doctor</u>, <u>female surgeon</u>, <u>lady</u> or <u>woman lawyer</u>. Those occupations with less social prestige must have a special "feminine" suffix attached to them, e.g., <u>waitress</u>, <u>authoress</u>, <u>poetess</u>, <u>majorette</u>. We understand any term that occurs in its "standard" unmarked form to refer to a male, and failure to provide the information that the person is a woman often results in confusion for the hearer. For example, if I tell a friend that I have an appointment with my lawyer/doctor/ therapist, she will assume that that person is male, and indicate that assumption by asking, "Oh, why are you going to see <u>him</u>?" or "Do you think <u>he</u> would see me?" In contrast, when a term is marked (+female) it acquires a negative connotation, the price exacted for moving out of our semantic space and into the domain of man. Those occupations ordinarily reserved for women, e.g., <u>prostitute</u>, <u>nurse</u>, secretary, teacher, require that the feature (+male) be marked explicitly, as in male nurse, male prostitute, male secretary. (There were fewer examples in this category since men have not shown as much interest in traditionally "female occupations" as women have shown in those of men, presumably because the jobs that women occupy pay less money.) That we need to mark occupational terms for gender indicates to me that our semantic space is rigidly determined by culturally defined sex roles, and when one of us goes beyond the boundary of the space provided for us by the English lexicon, we move into negative semantic space, and special linguistic accomodations must be made.

It is fair to ask at this point what the existence of special gender markers has to do with the question of generics in English. Just this: the place of women in our society is reflected in the semantic space that we occupy, a small space that contains such labels as prostitute, housewife, mother, nurse, and secretary; the remainder of the English semantic space, including those terms called "generics," belongs to the male sex. It would appear that the explicit semantic markers (+female) and (+male), are only the most obvious and superficial indicators of the way in which English semantic space, our cognitive space, reflects male dominance.

As I have said earlier, the arguments that favor man and man-kind as generics are not substantive, but political. The Oxford English Dictionary states clearly in its definitions of man that generic usage of the noun is "obsolete," and the editors go on to note that "in modern apprehension man as thus used primarily denotes the male sex, though by implication referring also to women" (my italics). Note that women are included in man only by implication, not inference! With respect to the phrase a man, the OED is equally explicit: The phrase is used "quasi-pronominally," for one, or any one, but it "implies a reference to the male sex only." And, as early as 1924, Otto Jespersen was blunt in his judgment that: "This is decidedly a defect in the English language," and he went on to mention that "the tendency recently has been to use unambiguous, if clumsy expressions like a human being . . ." (Jespersen, 1985: 231). Authorities notwithstanding, the men in the media have been making a lot of noise about recent attempts to alter or bypass the traditional masculine "generics," and their trivializations of the issues have taken various forms. In general, feminist suggestions have been put down and categorized as illicit tampering with the language, as fads, or as grotesque errors in a class with ain't and double negatives, depending upon the degree to which the writer identifies himself as the last bastion in defense of the "purity" of the English language. One writer has called feminist remodeling of the language "the new Sispeak" (Kanier, p. 79), while L.B. Sissman, in his article "Plastic English," says that such tampering is as threatening as the American Communist Party, and he accuses feminists of "distort(ing) and corrupt(ing) further the language already savaged by the Establishment politicians when they conspire to eliminate the innocuous, and correct, locution, 'Everyone knows he has to decide for himself,' and to substitute the odious Newspeakism 'chairperson' . . ." (Sissman, 1972: 37). Possibly the most recent example of the violent reactions to conscious language change were the letters written to the New York Times protesting the detailed and explicit

McGraw-Hill <u>Guidelines for the Equal Treatment of the Sexes</u>.

Men, however, are not the only ones resisting language change, nor are our opponents only the press pedagogues. Two women, Robin Lakoff and Alleen Pace Nilsen, are also opposed to eliminating masculine "generics," and their reasons are interesting for the insights they provide into the mechanisms of justification. Ms. Nilsen, although she suggests that we avoid terms like <u>man</u>, argues that "it is unrealistic to expect to get rid of all of them (generic masculine terms). Therefore, it makes more sense to adjust to them" (Nilsen, 1973: 9). The murkiness of this type of argument and the difficulty of rationalizing neutrality are illustrated in their concluding statement:

> Educational and psychological damage occurs only when people think that generic terms refer exclusively to males. And, unfortunately, rather than increasing awareness in the general public of the nature of the generic terms, the invention of specifically feminine terms such as <u>chairwoman</u>, <u>freshwoman</u>, <u>spokeswoman</u>, etc., has the opposite effect giving the impression that women cannot be included in any term incorporating a masculine marker. I fear that in the long run this will serve to exclude women even further from the mainstream of thought and action. (Nilsen, p. 10).

As I have already mentioned, generic terms <u>do</u> refer exclusively to males, except by implication, and Nilsen can only infer that she is included in them. But inference is not the same as denotation. The issue of "generic" has to do with what people think, and usage indicates that people think of a male when they write or hear man, except for those who have something invested in having us believe otherwise. For this reason, use of terms like chairwoman and spokeswoman are conscious choices and give us a social visibility in roles outside the home that we have never had, correctly asserting that women are not included in terms with masculine markers. Finally, if anything is likely to exclude women from worldly spheres, it will be the perpetuation of the notion that women are included in terms like forefather, or that high-sounding statements like "All men are created equal" or "God created man in his own image" include women as references.

Robin Lakoff's argument follows that of Nilsen in its studied neutrality, but Lakoff is not as careful in her assertions. While she is quite frank about her pessimism, counseling a conservative approach to conscious language change, she blithely accepts and supports the myth that "generics" refer to women as well as men, without consulting more carefully researched sources.

> . . . in English we find man and mankind, which of course refer to women members of the species as well. . . . but more seriously, I think one should force oneself to be realistic: certain aspects of language are available to the speaker's conscious analysis, and others are too common, too thoroughly mixed throughout the language, for the speaker to be aware each time he uses them. (Lakoff, 1975: 45)

Does Lakoff want us to believe that she was not conscious of it when she used the pronoun <u>he</u> in that last sentence? What is saddening about her statement is that she side-stepped the major issue she raised: It is precisely those aspects of language use that are not conscious that we have the most trouble eliminating from our speech. I cannot be satisfied with letting so-called generics continue to pass as such, just because some people do not want to think about what they're saying. One way of becoming aware of something is to talk about it, and to make our usage conscious. It would seem that as long as linguistic change is "accidental," linguists can afford to be nonchalant. But, in the cause of "political realism" we are cautioned to exert pressure on those areas of usage that are "available to the speaker's conscious analysis." Or, as Nilsen would have it, we need not be disturbed because "Educational and social damage occurs only when people think that the generic terms refer exclusively to males." If Nilsen is correct, then a great deal of educational and social damage has been done, especially in public school and college textbooks.

At this point we have no way of determining what is available to conscious analysis, nor can we ascertain when people think generic terms refer to women and men. Until further proof is forthcoming, it is safe to assume that so-called generics refer exclusively to the male sex, especially when the writer or speaker is male. In my opinion, women have wishfully read themselves into "generics" in an effort to remain ignorant of their political position. I am not speaking only of terms like <u>man</u> and <u>mankind</u>; such uses of masculine terms are too obvious to merit the attention given to them. I am saying that women have read themselves into other terms as well, for example, children, kids, people, person, individual, teacher, sociologist, and surgeon. As Otto Jespersen had observed:

> While a great many names for human beings are applicable to both sexes, e.g., liar, possessor, inhabitant, Christian, fool, stranger, neighbour, etc., others, though possessing no distinctive mark, are as a matter of fact chiefly or even exclusively applied to one sex only, because the corresponding social functions have been restricted either to men or to women. This is true of minister, bishop, lawyer, baker, shoemaker and many others on the one hand, nurse, dressmaker, milliner on the other (Jespersen, 1965: 232).

At the publication time of this article, things are pretty much the same.

The definitions that follow, taken from Random House Dictionary, make explicit the way in which the English lexicon is divided into two gender-determined vocabularies. The terms for which I have provided definitions are: feminine, womanly, and womanish; masculine, manly and mannish. The comments on effeminate were found under the definition for female. The two contrasting sets of terms delimit the semantic boundaries of "socially approved" behaviors we are expected to exhibit if we are unfortunate enough to have been born female or male.

FEMININE -- 1. Pertaining to a woman or girl: Feminine beauty, feminine dress. 2. Like a woman; weak; gentle.

WOMANLY -- Like or befitting a woman; feminine; not masculine or girlish. syn. -- WOMANLY implies resemblance in appropriate, fitting ways: WOMANLY DECORUM, MODESTY. WOMANLIKE, a neutral synonym, may suggest mild disapproval or, more rarely, disgust. WOMANLIKE, SHE(HE) BURST INTO TEARS. WOMANISH usually implies an inappropriate resemblance and suggests weakness or effeminacy: WOMANISH BEHAVIOR.

EFFEMINATE -- is applied reproachfully or contemptuously to qualities which, although natural in women, are seldom applied to women and are unmanly and weak when possessed by men: EFFEMINATE GESTURES; AN EFFEMINATE VOICE. FEMININE, corresponding to MASCULINE. Applies to the attributes particularly appropriate to women, esp. the softer and more delicate qualities. The word is seldom used to denote sex, and if applied to men, suggests the delicacy and weakness of women: A FEMININE FIGURE, POINT OF VIEW, FEATURES.

These definitions make explicit all of the cultural assumptions regarding the "true nature" of women: We are delicate, petulant, liable to burst into tears at any provocation, we possess decorum--have you ever heard of masculine decorum?--we are modest, we are weak, and we are gentle. Even the definitions of the terms for women are cast negatively, as that which is not masculine. Contrast the tone of these definitions with those for males, which are uniformly affirmative.

> MASCULINE -- 1. Having the qualities or characteristics of a man; manly; virile; strong; bold; A DEEP MASCULINE VOICE. 2. Pertaining to or characteristic of a man or men: MASCULINE ATTIRE.
>
> MANLY -- Having the qualities usually considered desirable in a man; strong; brave; honorable; resolute; virile. Syn. -- Manly implies possession of the most valuable or desirable qualities a man can have, as dignity, honesty, directness, etc., in opposition to servility, insincerity, underhandedness, etc. It also connotes strength, courage, and fortitude . . .

I infer from these definitions that women are servile, insincere, underhanded, weak, cowardly and lacking in fortitude. In fact, RHD offers as antonyms for manly three significant words: feminine; weak; cowardly. But the definition for mannish provides an exact illustration of what I have inferred from the previous definitions.

> MANNISH applies to that which resembles man: . . . applied to a woman, the term is derogatory, suggesting the aberrant possession of masculine characteristics.

Characteristics such as strength, dignity, honesty, and courage are "aberrant" in women!

The semantic space of English is neatly divided in accordance with social sex-role stereotypes; women are fragile, passive and dishonest, all negative attributes, whereas men are strong, bold, honest and forthright, all positive attributes. In the examples that follow, we can see ways in which the stereotypes of women are taken for granted in various media, with the understanding that the characteristics of women are negative in comparison to the positive standards set for men.

1) A. The guards were seldom harsh and never cruel. They tended to be stolid, slovenly, heavy, and to my eyes, effeminate -- not in the sense of delicacy, etc., but in just the opposite sense: a gross, bland fleshiness, a bovinity without point or edge. Among my fellow-prisoners I had also for the first time in Winter the sense of being a man among women, or among eunuchs. The prisoners were hard to tell apart; their emotional tone seemed always low, their talk trivial. (Ursula K. LeGuin, The Left Hand of Darkness, p. 170)

B. Ignorant, in the Handdarn sense: To ignore the abstraction, to hold fast to the thing. There was in this attitude something feminine, a refusal of the abstract, the ideal, a submissiveness to the given, which rather displeased me. (LeGuin, The Left Hand of Darkness, Pp. 202-203)

C. Every man's been one, every woman's had one. (Ad for the movie, Paperback Hero)

D. Is there a lady in the house, with some children and a spouse, with some worries on her mind about dinner?
(Radio ad, Athens, Georgia)

E. Usually, however, role analysis is pitched in terms of the roles of some particular category of person, such as doctor or female. (Erving Goffman, Encounters, p. 91)

F. Gibson's has special bargains for the ladies: 40% off on clothes for children, and double sheets, two for the price of one.
(Radio ad, Athens, Georgia)

G. It is a far cry from the unfortunate days when slaps and kicks were exchanged, weak sisters exploded in tears, and strong men staged walkouts. (Judith Crist, New York, 1/20/75, p. 50)

Each of these examples illustrates the type of context in which we find reference to women, and the use of traditional concepts of women and their behavior, as further explanation is unnecessary. I could multiply these examples, but I offer them only as evidence that the polarization of roles defined by terms like feminine and masculine can be found in contexts in which the words themselves need not appear. The contexts in 1.A. - 1.G. demonstrate the strength and prevalence of sexist assumptions in our society; one need only call upon them to sell sheets, promote a movie, describe an alien personality, or outline a method of role analysis in which one has doctors, on the one hand, and females on the other.

The next set of examples contains explicit references to women. The topic in each quotation, whether it is food, motherhood or embroidery, is one assumed to be of interest only to women. Consequently, I would like to emphasize the terms that do not appear; we do not find the "generic" man, although, if we remember our traditional grammar, we learned that any group that contained one male had to be referred to by a masculine generic. The writer of each example, then, must assume that no single male is interested in food, embroidery, crafts, or reproduction. Nor do we find person, people, or individual, terms that would theoretically include women.

    2) A. As Woman, she would have been happier had she continued enshrined in the privacy of domestic love and domestic duty. (Frank Caprio, Female Homosexuality)

        B. This comprehensive book of one hundred embroidery stitches will be useful not only to teachers and students, but to women of all ages who are interested in embroidery stitches. (100 Embroidery Stitches, p. 2)

C. Women unconsciously prefer to fulfill their maternal role and to be loved by a man. Woman is intended for reproduction. (Caprio, *Female Homosexuality*)

D. The right idea for today's creative woman from the Cooking and Crafts Club. (Book-of-the-Month Club Flyer)

When the subject matter pertains to one of those categories that fall within the semantic space of women, we will find the term *woman*, and *not* a masculine generic. Notice, however, that when the topic falls within the semantic space reserved for male behaviors and male concerns, such as anger, control, autonomy or dignity, we find the so-called generics *man* and *mankind*.

3. A. By questioning the control exercised by autonomous man and demonstrating the control exercised by the environment, a science of behavior also seems to question dignity or worth. (B.F. Skinner, *Beyond Freedom and Dignity*)

B. A small step for man, a giant step for mankind! (Astronaut)

C. The history of anger is the history of mankind. Man has been exposed to the effects of anger, others' as well as his own, since he was first placed on earth. (*Anger*, p. 1)

Before I go on to consider the problem of reference with respect to terms of more general application, I would like to offer for your consideration a set of anomalous examples, anomalous because of the semantic ambiguities and shifts of reference which they illustrate.

4. A. Man is not made for defeat... A man can be destroyed but not defeated.
(Hemingway, <u>The Old Man and the Sea</u>)

B. Archeologists announced today that they have discovered evidence of man's existence as far back as 3,000,000 years ago, based on the dating of a woman's skeleton.
(Radio news, Knoxville)

C. A college professor had dinner at the home of her department chairman. After dinner, he invited her to join him in his study, and his wife invited her to watch TV in the livingroom. Her chairman prevailed in the awkward debate that followed, insisting that they needed the privacy. As the two of them were entering his study, his daughter followed them in, wanting to know <u>why</u> the professor had to stay with him in is study.
"Because," replied the father, "that's what the men do." (private conversation)

And one finds interesting extensions of the masculine bias with the verb <u>to man</u>, in spite of the OED's definition, "to fill with men." The following anecdote illustrates how far some are willing to push for the genericness of the male norm.

  D. In a midwestern college, a memorandum was circulated informing the faculty that the registration tables would have to "be manned." When a woman pointed out that half of the department was women, her chairman replied: "You're a man. The Bible says 'In the beginning God created man in his own image.' So, God created you and you're a man." (Private correspondence)

I wish I could leave you with the obvious ways in which women are excluded from semantic space beyond that occupied by their traditional roles. By now, the appeal to the genericness of masculine terms may seem hardly noteworthy. But my last set of examples, uses terms of general reference, e.g., <u>person</u>, <u>child</u>, <u>kid</u>, and <u>individual</u>, provide evidence that whenever someone speaks or writes about "people," the intended reference of the given term is males.

 5) A. You're a mother and a wife, and your <u>men</u> count on you. So take One-a-Day Vitamins with iron for the <u>people</u> who count on you. (Television ad)

  B. <u>First Satirist</u>: A satirist can't teach <u>people</u> anything if he offends <u>them</u>. <u>Second Satirist</u>: I offend <u>them</u>. <u>They</u> love it. I make fun of <u>their</u> wives. (Jules Feiffer, <u>Feiffer's Album</u>, p. 2)

C. Our <u>people</u> are the best gamblers in the galaxy. <u>We</u> compete for power, fame, women. (<u>Star Trek</u>)

D. Jack thought with surprise how good this was. This atmosphere of dim, shabby <u>people</u>, <u>men</u> who would not recognize him or anything in him. . (Joyce Carol Oates, <u>Do With Me What You Will</u>, p. 517-518)

E. When I was going to school, I spent most of my time talking to <u>teachers</u> and <u>their</u> wives. (Edward Albee, in an interview, <u>New Yorker</u>, 6/8/74, p. 29)

F. For the merry-go-round rider, for example, the <u>self</u> awaiting is one that entails a child's portion of bravery and muscular control, a <u>child's</u> portion of <u>manliness</u> . . . (Goffman, <u>Encounters</u>, p. 98)

G. American middle-class <u>two-year olds</u> often find the prospect too much for <u>them</u>. <u>They</u> fight <u>their</u> parents at the last moment to avoid being strapped into a context in which it had been hoped <u>they</u> would be little <u>men</u> (Goffman, <u>Encounters</u>, p. 105)

H. We find that <u>holders of the MA and MS</u> who enter this department do well in graduate work here. <u>Their</u> applications, like those of women, and of members of minority groups, are welcome. (Dept. of Psychology flyer, U-T Knoxville)

I. Even in the most serious of roles, such as that of _surgeon_, we yet find that there will be times when the full-fledged _performer_ must unbend and behave simply as a _male_. (Goffman, _Encounters_, p. 140)

J. This kind of equipment is to the _homecraftsman_ what washing machines, clothes dryers, etc. . . . are to the housewife. (_Woodworking_)

K. It is here, in this personal capacity, that an _individual_ can be warm, spontaneous, and touched by humor. It is here, regardless of _his_ social role, that an _individual_ can show "what kind of a guy he is." (Goffman, _Encounters_, p. 152)

L. _Sociologists_ _qua_ _sociologists_ are allowed to have one profane part; _sociologists_ _qua_ _persons_, along with other _persons_, retain the sacred for _their_ friends, _their_ wives, and _themselves_. (Goffman, _Encounters_, p. 152)

M. Ordinary walking may have to be put on, too, especially, presumably, by the half of our population whose appearance is, and is designed to be, appreciated by <u>all</u>, and savored by <u>some</u>, . . .(Goffman, <u>Relations in Public</u>, p.272)

Each of the preceding examples illustrates how completely women are excluded from the semantic space occupied by masculine definitions, through either a specifically male term, e.g., <u>manly</u>, <u>manliness</u>, <u>men</u>, or an explicitly female reference, e.g., <u>wives</u>, <u>mother</u>, <u>housewife</u>. Such usage provides some evidence that women are rarely, if ever, present as persons in a writer's mind, which, in its turn, tells us how far we have yet to go in exposing sexism to "conscious analysis." The varied sources for these examples also provide us with an index of the "educational and social damage" done to women in the media. In addition, the obvious prevalence of male referents for terms that are generally defined as neutral with respect to gender calls into question the validity of Lakoff's claim that nouns like <u>person</u> and <u>people</u> are "purely empty" (Lakoff, 1975: 37).

Where does one go from here? What are we to do when we have to continue to use a language in which semantic space is dominated by males? For the time being, I suggest that we mark gender explicitly, creating pairs of terms, e.g., <u>chairwoman/chairman</u>, <u>spokeswoman/spokesman</u>, <u>saleswoman/salesman</u>. The use of neutralized terms perpetuates the invisibility of women in positions outside their traditionally defined roles, and the tendency to assume that such roles are filled by males has been illustrated earlier in this paper. Our language is sexist because our society is sexist, and until there is significant reversal of the prevalent attitudes toward women we cannot hope to accomplish much. As Lakoff has observed: "The presence of the words is a signal that something is wrong, rather than (as too often interpreted by well-meaning reformers) the problem itself" (p. 21). Nevertheless, efforts to remove biased gender reference from our vocabulary may at least force upon us an awareness of the deeply ingrained sexism that usage reflects.

Gender Bias as a Threat to Construct Validity in Research Design

Judith A. Levy

Reflexive Statement

This paper examines how gender bias common to the domain assumptions, language structures, and interpretive processes of research confound a study's construct validity. My purpose in selecting this topic is to show how science's traditional theoretical and methodological treatment of women compromises study results. The issues presented here are familiar to feminists and other concerned scholars. My intent is to show how these issues impact upon study design. I have chosen to focus on construct validity because it plays a critical role in determining what "facts" get accepted as reality (Kerlinger, 1964).

Science as a Social Product

Science operates as a social enterprise governed by a system of rules and assumptions reflecting the values of a larger social order (Sjoberg, 1975). Within the production of knowledge known as research, scientists serve as the mediating link between a society's normative structure and what becomes legitimated as fact. Like all people, scientists come to know and make sense of the world they encounter through a set of culturally defined understandings and proscriptions. Despite attempts to limit their influence, these orientations enter into the research process through the investigator's preconceptions of how the world does or should operate (Burtt, 1946). Moreover, science itself consists of a sequence of emergent and competing truth-paradigms that limit human inquiry to a narrow range of topics and beliefs (Kuhn, 1970). Thus, the very questions that scientists pose, the indicators that they select, the designs that they choose, and the conclusions that they draw have their conceptual origins in the moral ethics and body of knowledge deemed important by a particular society or scientific community (Weber, 1947; Nadel, 1951; Sjoberg, 1975).

In challenging the myth of a value-free science, a number of scholars have taken a critical look at how scientific inquiry reflects and is used to reinforce the interests and preconceptions of its producers (see Hubbard, et al., 1979). Given that scientific work traditionally has been the prerogative of males (Vetter, 1976; Kelly-Gadol, 1976) and that women's lives and experiences have been judged as less important than those of men (Acker, 1973), it is not surprising that a strong androcentric bias in theory, language, and methods has been uncovered. Recognition that science through its findings both contributes to and legitimates male supremacy presents feminists and other concerned scholars with a difficult question (Keller, 1982): Can one be both feminist and scientist without sacrificing either one's moral or ethical beliefs?

One pathway through the dilemma lies in integrating a feminist consciousness with the methods and principles of dominant science. This objective requires continued effort to examine the theory and methods of science to identify gender-centered biases and to substitute these conventions with a value-neutral form. As a solution, this action neither surrenders the rewards and opportunities of participation in mainstream science nor abandons a vulnerable public to knowledge or social policies based upon androcentric truths. As this paper addresses the research dangers of unacknowledged prejudice, let me state quite clearly that my own preference toward resolving the feminist-scholar's quandary lies in scientific reform.

The following discussion of gender bias as a threat to construct validity represents a step toward this goal. Too often, women's criticism of sexism in research gets sloughed aside by the nonsympathetic as another instance of "women bitching about nothing." My underlying argument is that producing higher study validity through elimination of androcentric bias should be of concern to anyone who values the integrity of his or her research. Based upon this premise, I begin my analysis by examining the politics of validity as a social construct.

Validity as a Social Construct

For many years, discussion of a study's validity centered on two concerns. Content validity assessed the representativeness or sampling adequacy of a measuring instrument by asking if all items or components of a phenomenon had been included. Predictive validity (also known as criterion validity) referred to the extent to which an instrument could predict a particular behavior or outcome. Neither form, however, was concerned with an instrument's adequacy for explaining why a functional relationship might exist between variables.

Around the 1950s, <u>construct validity</u> was added to the list (Nunnally and Durham, 1975). Considered the most important of the three forms of validity, here concern centers on "the approximate" validity with which one can make generalizations about higher order constructs from research operations (Cook and Campbell, 1979: 38). Construct validity is established by ruling out rival hypotheses known as "threats to validity" created through operational bias. Such threats are what experimentalists mean when they speak of confounding factors.

Constructs themselves are heuristic devices developed by scientists to describe and measure abstract variables. The term validity is a construct, as are the terms gender, feminine, nurturing, instinct, and Oedipal complex. Constructs, rather than specific variables, are the building blocks of research in that they represent half-formed theoretical assumptions about how a variety of behaviors correlate (Nunnally and Durham, 1975). It is important to stress that constructs exist nowhere except within the theory and imagination of their producers.

As social products, constructs are both creations and reflections of scientific training, theory and the personal biases of their originators; and as social products, invalid constructs have contributed to and helped to perpetuate many common stereotypes and misconceptions about men and women. Gender bias enters into the development of constructs at three critical points: when specifying the domain of variables that form a construct, when developing the language structures used to establish functional relationships, and during research operations. Each of these junctures merits closer inspection.

Domain Assumptions

Although constructs are abstract notions, they are made concrete through operational definitions which specify those phenomena from a domain of observables believed to be related to the construct. The process of determining which variables do or do not belong to a particular domain long has been recognized as critical to limiting measurement error. What seldom gets acknowledged, however, is that constructs themselves form definitions of reality with the power to order experience into their framework. For example, when Freud declared the clitoral orgasm as an indication of the construct "infantile personality," this domain assumption coerced several generations of women into seeking more "mature" (but nonexistent) vaginal variety (see Koedt, 1973). Thus, one danger with constructs is that they sometimes shape rather than help to explain reality.

The constructed realities that emerge through the specification of constructs are a direct function of the social relations embedded in the production of knowledge. Historically and into the present, science predominately has been a male enterprise with women accorded a marginal role (Hughes, 1975; Daniels, 1975). This male domination has resulted in the limiting of scientific inquiry to the study of what males do and what men value largely to the exclusion of topics and research problems pertaining directly to women (Bernard, 1973). In examining the classical theory, for example, we find that Weber's exploration of the constructs of "bureaucracy," "power," and "authority" involve the rationalization of labor in a work sphere dominated by men and only incidentally populated by women. This neglect of women's experience as a potential for study continues into the present. Contemporary social science has yet to produce a comprehensive body of knowledge that adequately represents female participation within the formal organization and structuring of work (Kanter, 1977).

In following this example further, we find that as a male enterprise, science has failed to create a viable scheme of economic valuation that includes nonpaid labor of the sort that women typically perform. This inadequacy is well illustrated by the economic construct "Gross National Product" which excludes output from household labor as a measure of a nation's productivity. Under this theoretical accounting system, the woman who leaves paid employment to care for her family actually withdraws wealth from society.

When translated into public policy, such limited constructs generate problems in national planning because they do not represent the larger reality or even prove satisfactorily pragmatic. The Social Security Administration, for example, has struggled for years with the problem of evaluating women's retirement benefits accrued through their husband's earnings. Disability entitlements entail similar difficulties. Some analysts have followed the policy of equating the earnings of a housewife with that of a domestic servant or with the replacement value of hiring someone from the labor force (Cooper and Rice,

1976). Others have assigned dollar value to housework and child care based upon the average wage lost by an individual due to working at home (Weisbrod, 1961; Gronau, 1973). These measures, which rely upon contorted reasoning to salvage their underlying constructs, are widely recognized as being inadequate. When used for cost-benefit purposes and other forms of quantitatively based policy decisions, household and other nonsalary workers of either sex are less likely to be targeted for human capital investment or to benefit from disability transfer programs than those gainfully employed (Nobel, 1977; Murdrick, 1983).

Three points emerge from such observations. First, valid constructs cannot be built without considering how the social production of science lends itself to the selection of certain phenomena or theoretical perspectives for study over other research possibilities. This selection process extends to the specification of variables and to the domain assumptions which form a study's theoretical constructs. Given the patriarchal division of labor common to both society and science, one need ask only "Cui bono?" to understand how few incentives exist for a male enterprise to ask questions or to consider viewpoints that represent the social realities of other claimants. Thus, valid constructs only emerge as competing paradigms offer conflict and challenge. As new groups of people move into science, the opportunity for innovation and improved understandings increases (Millman and Kanter, 1975).

Second, through critical analysis of the social structure, it has become increasingly clear that women, minorities, the disabled and many other subgroups of people inhabit social and symbolic worlds not represented by the life experiences or opportunity structures relevant to white males. Thus, as Smith (1974a) observes, the formers' experiences, attitudes and life-paths cannot be understood by using the theoretical and methological schemata that explain, reproduce and legitimate the social relations serving the latter. The fact is, we still know very little about the private, unofficial and informal worlds that exist outside a male-defined division of labor (Millman and Kanter, 1975). Furthermore, opportunities for insight and exploration into the rich variation of human experience have been lost through science's reliance upon white and middle-class males to serve as the normative proxy for all categories of people.

Finally, we still know very little about the similarities and differences that characterize the two sexes despite researchers' frequent and typically unquestioning use of sex as an explanatory variable. This lack of information is compounded by general disagreement among researchers over the basic concepts central to gender research. The problem manifests itself in arguments over which sets of phenomena differentiate "masculine" from "feminine" and "sex" from "gender."

Despite continuing controversy and confusion, the term "sex" commonly is used in science when referring to biological characteristics like chromosonal, physiological and hormonal structures (Walum, 1977). This convention is based upon the assumption that genital and reproductive structures are both discernable and nonambiguous. By extension, the terms "masculine" and "feminine" are used when referring to dimorphic differences at the psychological level. "Gender," meanwhile, typically refers to the cognitive, social and cultural aspects of masculine and feminine social roles. All three constructs are characterized as being bipolar and dichotomous. While these assumptions lend themselves to the building of parsimonious models and seemingly straight-forward coding schemes, the world is really far more complex than these "either/or" maxims suggest.

One of the major problems in defining sex as a dichotomous variable is that biological structures are inconsistent. Hermaphrodites, for example, manifest both male and female sex organs, a circumstance that is celebrated in some societies (Tressemer, 1975b). Similarly, under the Eve Principle, a person can have the chromosonal pattern (xy) of a male but the anatomical structure of a female. To complicate things further, both men and women produce male hormones (androgen and testosterone) and female hormones (estrogen and progesterone) with some individuals manufacturing more of the cross-sex hormone than their own (Walum, 1977). Meanwhile, a person's gender identity, role enactment, or sexual preference may run counter to the cultural norm.

Such confusion prompted Kessler and McKenna (1978) to observe that people (including researchers) seldom are in the position to know the genital/reproductive structure of another person or where social and biological contradictions might be at work. Rather, sex and gender assignments are typically made on the basis of the person's self report, appearance, demeanor, personality and so forth. I would hasten to add that, while this practice may prove satisfactory in social encounters, precepts founded upon erroneous assumptions reinforce misconceptions and invalidate research findings when appropriated for scientific purposes. This caveat, then, raises an important question: How should investigators handle sex and gender differences on the conceptual and operational level when designing research?

While the answer may appear deceptively simple, better research constructs begin with the recognition that there is more to sex and gender than is first apparent. While undoubtedly most research will continue to use sex as a dichotomous variable, the possibilities for new understandings extend with the acknowledgement that dimorphism is a convention of probability and convenience, not irrefutable fact. Moreover, masculine and feminine need to be recognized as separate and multi-dimensional traits shared by all human beings with much individual variation. Personal characteristics like race, ethnicity, social class and physical disability further influence an individual's role performance. Such interactional effects should be taken into account when specifying constructs. Finally, constructs and other forms of counterproductive thinking which artificially widen the differences between the sexes need to be eliminated (Tressemer, 1975a; 1975b). To explore this last point further, let us turn to how the language of science, through the explication of constructs, accords men superiority over women.

Language Structures

The adequate specification of a construct requires the precise delineation of its terms and operations. As

Cook and Campbell (1979:65) observe, this precision "is vital for high construct validity because it permits tailoring the manipulations and measures to whichever definitions emerge from the explication." Given the importance that researchers attach to finely specified contructs, it is very revealing to examine how traditional science has dealt with constructs pertaining to women. Let us consider, for a moment, the relationship between science and language.

Chung (1970) observes that the philosophy and methods of Western science are drawn primarily from the principles of Aristotelian logic with its subject-predicate form of language structure. The verbs "to be" and "it is" which make up the basic units of Western syntax, are a direct legacy of Greek philosophical conclusions concerning the nature of human existence and matter. The very notion of causality rests upon identifying discrete categories of phenomena, then specifying relationships between them. Thus, Western logic can be seen as "identity logic" and Western science as the process of naming and placement within a framework of theory, concepts and assumptions.

But if the logic of science can be seen as conforming to the laws of identity, then women as a social category have held an ambiguous and often invisible position within this scientific ordering. I refer especially to how science traditionally has condoned and even actively encouraged researchers to use male terms when referring specifically to males and generically to human beings. Thus, to use a well known example, anthropologists refer to the evolution of early man as if it were accomplished without early woman; sociologists study the relationships of man to society; and psychologists look to the problem of man against himself. Meanwhile, the use of "he" when also meaning "she" renders both women and their experiences as socially invisible amd powerless. It seems, then, that the careful explication of terms and constructs, so vital to establishing functional relationships within research, does not extend to recognize women as active and highly visible participants in society.

The language of science neutralizes women's lives and experiences in a second pervasive and far-reaching way. Hanson (1965) notes that causal connections are only possible in language which is multi-level in explanatory power. While the world can be described through sense-datum words like "red," "wet" or "high," these expressions lack the explanatory power necessary to envision functional relationships. The latter activity requires certain theory-laden words that connote power or direction. Examples drawn from physics include the terms "force," "momentum," "mass," "velocity" and "reaction."

When theory and sense-datum words become linked, they form the cause and effect patterns of a causal relationship. Based upon one's theory or view of the world, certain sequences of pair- words tend to appear repeatedly together. "Rain stops" commonly is associated with "sun's out," "pin pricks--baby cries," "door slams--cake falls." Herein lies the potential for research bias.

The language relevant in discussions of reproductive biology offers an excellent example of how invalid causal relationships get established. In describing "coitus," for instance, the male term is paired with words like "erection," "penetration," "excitement" and "aggression"; female, on the other hand, pairs with "congestion," "reception," "reticence" and "passivity." The effect is to "animate" men and "deanimate" women while suggesting women play a passive part in human conception (Hersberger, 1984). The linking of pair words shows similar androcentrism. Consider for example the typical biological sequence "sperm swims--penetrates egg." Now compare it with a more estrocentric (woman-centered) pattern: "egg lures--engulfs sperm." While the latter form, or better yet, a more neutral description, might more aptly describe the uniting of ovum and sperm, scientists under the guise of objectivity perpetuate a language convention in which males act on females. Similar examples of causal bias created through theoretical constructs appear throughout the physical and social sciences (Hubbard, 1979).

A third way that language structure contributes to distorted images of women occurs through misappropriation of constructs from other disciplines. Reductionism argues that the laws, theories and concepts formulated in one branch of science can be fruitfully transposed to another branch of science. One of the attractions of reductionist thinking is that it provides the isomorphic mechanism necessary to justify belief in the unity of science.

Reductionism has proven particularly popular among researchers interested in applying the findings from studies of animal behavior to human beings. Nonhuman primates have received close attention because they are thought to represent a simpler version of human beings untouched by the influence of culture. Perhaps not surprisingly, primates are found to organize themselves according to psycho-biological drives that designate males as dominant and aggressive while females are protrayed as submissive and nurturing. In describing the behavior of chimpanzees, for example, males are said to "mount," females are described as "receptive"; males "demand" and females "demure"; males "hunt" and females "forage" (Herschberger, 1954). If these descriptions begin to sound like the pair-words we just encountered, it is not by coincidence. The upshot of such reductionism is to suggest that the natural order of humans, like primates and some other animals, genetically is predisposed to a social organization in which males assume the role obligations and privileges of leadership.

Leaving aside the political implications of reductionist thinking, the principle has been strongly criticized on methodological grounds. One drawback is that reductionism can lead to erroneous conclusions by confusing concepts with process. For instance, while both might be accurately described by the construct "courtship," dating behavior in human beings takes a special form and meaning not replicated within the ritualized mating patterns of elks or loons. Furthermore, the uncritical application of lower animal behavior to human beings denies the powerful influence of culture in reshaping patterns of behavior. Researchers, then, would be well advised to proceed cautiously when building reductionist assumptions into research theory and design.

Operational Bias

The confounding of constructs on a theoretical level has its parallel in the selection of design and operations. Since the Hawthorne studies first pointed to research subjects as active participants shaping the research process, it has become increasingly clear that how data are collected affects subject behavior and the relationships which get expressed between variables. To offset contextual effects, research ideally should triangulate measures and methods to reduce measurement error. That is, evidence gained independently from multiple sources and through multiple measures should converge upon the construct to indicate the same or similar results. At the same time, data collected through numerous studies and under varying conditions should yield the same meanings and comparable findings (Campbell and Fiske, 1959).

Unfortunately, investigations that bring together information describing how males and females may respond according to differing social circumstance are sadly lacking in the literature. What little is known about contextual influences must be pieced together from a few diverse and isolated research clues. Girls may score higher on intelligence tests when the test is administered by a woman (Pederson, et al., 1975); some men misrepresent their attitudes toward women when they believe their falsehoods will not be detected (Hough and Bem, 1975); and both sexes appear to avoid success when they perceive that winning will have negative consequences (Tressemer, 1974b).

Such findings point to the need for research methods that consider the "situated aspects" of human behavior (Denzin, 1978). Scientific fact is produced within a social context that elicits situation-specific responses.

This circumstantial nature of self and its disclosure is true whether data are collected through paper and pencil tests, observational methods or tightly controlled experimental design. Construct validity improves as possible sources of operational bias are identified and then eliminated. As Cook and Campbell (1979) deal with such techniques at length, I leave it to them to outline the necessary procedures. Instead, let us consider "experimenter expectancy" as it affects research results and interpretations. I will focus on Terman's (1925) testing of the variability hypothesis because it illustrates the personal difficulties frequently encountered in relinquishing one's a priori assumptions.

The variability hypothesis dates from the turn of the century when Darwin's theory of species variation became popular among the general public and scientists alike. This thesis asserts that males are more likely than females to vary from the norm and that this distribution follows a normal curve. It implies that while men may be represented by a greater number of undesirable traits, they also have the greater capacity for genius and physical excellence. Despite almost a century of research devoted to proving the hypothesis, little evidence has been found to support these assertions (Shields, 1982).

While historically interesting, evidence for or against the variability hypothesis would not be of direct concern to construct validity were it not for the interpretive process through which researchers frame their results. Instead, theories, perspectives, hypotheses and constructs function as ideological structures "lending evidence to" or "failing to support" certain assumptions.

A persistent threat to research validity occurs where investigators became so inured with their own theories that they reinterpret study findings to fit these preconceptions.

Terman's (1925) attempt to verify the variability hypothesis through a study of gifted children offers a case in point. The study consisted of children nominated by their teachers as being especially bright. Although girls achieved the highest IQ scores, Terman (1925: 54) concluded that the results were "in harmony with the hypothesis that conceptually superior intelligence occurs with greater frequency among boys than girls." The rationale? Despite the likelihood of subject-selecting bias, Terman pointed to the larger number of boys nominated to the sample as proof of male superiority. In doing so, he sidestepped his own findings in order to focus on an aspect of his methods which might salvage his working hypotheses. Lest we make Terman the sole culprit in such deeds, however, it is important to point out that the variability hypothesis has received similar interpretive treatment from a number of investigators (see Shields, 1982). Furthermore, Terman himself acknowledged his mistake as data accumulated to suggest other interpretations.

Nonetheless, the common pattern of such studies is that over the years, they tend to form what Busch (1980) refers to as the "sedimentary structure" of a discipline or paradigm. This term suggests that much like the earth's geophysical crust, scientific knowledge develops through a layering process in which successive studies build upon the findings of earlier work. At the lower strata are the studies which provide the taken-for-granted assumptions of a discipline. These investigations may go unchallenged though their study methods or conclusions are faulty. Threats to the construct validity of other studies arise when these failings become codified within a popular scale, instrument or study design. The challenge for all researchers lies in ferreting out such instances of dated and biased thinking to produce more valid and useful alternatives.

Conclusions

This paper began by questioning whether science and feminism are compatible. The answer, as I see it, lies in bringing a feminist consciousness to mainstream research to produce a new mode of science. This task requires not only the reexamination of science to uncover male bias, but also the thoughtful formulation of new structures which incorporate valuable and valid elements of the old. But in doing so, we must guard against righting past grievances by introducing new constructs which unfairly disadvantage males or contribute to an estrocentric bias. This latter ideology would be as pernicious to truth as male belief systems have proven.

In examining construct validity, I have focused primarily on the formation and specification of constructs. Scientific progress depends less on the accumulation of new facts or discoveries than on developing constructs with better explanatory and predictive power. It is here, within the theoretical and abstract notions of how the world is organized, that feminism, through its sensitive and collective experience, can contribute greatly to new insights and better understandings.

ACKNOWLEDGEMENT

I would like to thank Mary Jo Deegan, Jane Ollenburger and Gary Albrecht for their comments on earlier versions of the paper. Also, Gwendolyn Slaughter and Susan Buss for their help in preparing the final draft.

Sociology of Medicine for Whom?: Feminist Perspectives in a Multi-Paradigmatic Sociology of Medicine

Juanne N. Clark

Reflexive Statement

My mother was a nurse, always called on when the neighbor's child fell out of a high chair, woke up with spots or red eyes, or had a fever. But, like others with whom I've talked whose parents offer health care services, I learned to feel that sickness was a weakness. I grew to feel ashamed of being sick; to have to rationalize and justify my own indisposition or to ignore or hide it. Through this, I learned that sickness and health were not biological events only but were constructed out of a web of social relations and meanings. And I developed an interest in the social-psychological aspects of health and illness. Later, I was swept away with feminist awareness and concerns and asked myself in what ways women and men and health and illness intersected. From these experiences and my academic education came thoughts such as those explored in this paper.

Feminist Perspectives in the Sociology of Medicine

On the one hand, this chapter discusses the interaction of two sets of interests: feminism and medical sociology. On the other hand, it argues that sociology must acknowledge its divergent roots. The traditions of the classic theorists Marx, Durkheim, and Weber have spearheaded widely different schools in sociology (Ritzer, 1975; Boughey, 1978; Sherman, 1974; and Mullins, 1973). These are believed, by their firmest adherents, to be both theoretically and methodologically distinct from one another and incompatible. This tenet has considerable political influence. Publications, research monies, appointments, conference themes, and policy suggestions are firmly constrained by theory affiliation. The correct epistemological assumptions about the science of the social world lead to adherence to one group or another. One purpose of this chapter is to clarify the multi-paradigmatic nature of sociology of medicine and to discuss some of the strengths and weaknesses of each paradigm. The other interest this paper addresses is women and the social sciences. A multi-paradigmatic sociology must include considerations of theoretical and methodological issues which have been raised by feminist sociologists, for example, Millman and Kanter (1975), Ehrenreich and English (1978), and Roberts (1981). Each of these authors' critiques are discussed more specifically here.

Millman and Kanter (1975) argue that a feminist consciousness would alter the course of conventional sociology. They distinguish six crucial changes:

1) New non-sexist subject areas and models would be revealed;

2) The focus on the public, official, and visible would be minimized in favour of the informal, invisible, and private;

3) The distinct social worlds of men and women would be recognized;

4) Sex itself would be taken into account as a factor in social behavior;

5) Radical transformation and change of the social order would be emphasized; and

6) New methodologies would emerge.

Feminist sociology would have an impact, therefore, on each of the major paradigms examined here.

Ehrenreich and English's work reorients analysis in the sociology of medicine to consider ways in which both health and medical definitions and institutions are constructs of sexist medical and sociological practice (see Clarke, 1983, for an examination of this phenomenon in a decade review of the literature on gender and illness).

Roberts (1981b) directs our attention to feminist and non-sexist methodologies which advocate the necessity of taking both men and women into explict account as subjects of a study and as researchers:

> Feminist research, then, is concerned not only with making women visible, but with theoretical and methodological issues, with problems of sexual divisions in the research team and the research process, and with the language of research findings

and the ways in which these may be used when they are published (1981b: 26).

Feminist scholars have looked beyond the order of sexism, though, and examined similar biases with respect to the tendency to assume homogeneity amongst subjects and researchers with respect to racial or ethnic background, social class, and sexual preference (personal communication with Deegan and Moore, 1984).

Women are the major producers and the consumers of health care (Douyal, 1979). Their position in the health care system, however, mirrors their position in society. When women are the subjects of investigation, it is most often as patients rather than as doctors or nurses (Lorber, 1975). They are powerless, the deprived. The classification of women as sick is the result of a double jeopardy. They are diagnosed by white, middle-class, male physicians and sociologists (Blishen, 1969, 1976; Scully, 1980; Clarke, 1983). Women's work in the health care system is relatively ignored, and they play comparatively powerless and economically deprived roles as nurses, nurse's aides, and nurse's assistants (Navarro, 1975). Lorber summarized these problems in her title: "Women and Medical Sociology: Invisible Professionals and Ubiquitous Patients."

Paradigmatic Analysis

The next section of this chapter describes each paradigm, presents an exemplar of each paradigm, and offers a feminist critique.

Positivism

The fundamental assumption of the positivst position is that the purpose of sociology is to understand--using the techniques and methods of the physical sciences--how order in a society is maintained. Thus, the roles of men and women in the structured institution of medicine become worthy subjects of investigation. Knowledge is power because knowledge provides an understanding of the present and permits prediction of the future. Social order is to be explained and the future predicted by means of a series of "if x, then y" statements. Two variables, statistically verified and in predictive relationships, form the building blocks of this positivist edifice. All levels of analysis are encompassed. Theories of the middle range, as well as micro-level and macro-level theories, are appropriate.

Talcott Parsons' (1951) work is the germinal work in the positivist paradigm. Theoretically, this work is labelled structural functionalist. Often it is of such a high order of generality and abstraction that it is impossible to empirically investigate. For example, in the discussion of both patients and the professions, Parsons ignores the relevance of sex, gender, class, race, and sexual preference. Sickness is a role, played alike by persons of both genders, all classes, ethnic groups, races, ages, and sexual preferences. When people become ill, they adopt a specific sick role that has four features:

1) Sick persons are not held responsible for their incapacity;

2) They are exempted from their usual role and task obligations;

3) They must want to leave the role and get well; and

4) They are obliged to seek and comply with technically competent medical advice.

All these conditions are assumed to be relevant for everyone.

Empirical literature (again, in a positivist tradition) has shown that these expectations are not the same for everyone. Men and women, for instance, are likely to differ in some crucial ways that are relevant to the sick role analysis. In the first place, women, particularly those of certain classes, ethnic and racial backgrounds (Ehrenreich and English, 1978), are widely believed by doctors to be _more responsible_ for their own illnesses than men. Women are believed to be victimized by their emotions and to be more likely to suffer psychosomatic illnesses. Their reproductive organs are considered to be the origin of unpredictable and irresponsible behaviour (Lorber, 1975; Ehrenreich & English, 1973a, 1973b; Chesler, 1972). Second, sick days, with or without pay, are not as easily available to women who work in jobs with hourly or low wages--as a large number of women do at present (McDonald, 1975; and Himelfarb and Richardson, 1982). Because of the relatively isolated nuclear family, it is difficult for a sick woman to receive exemption from everyday role and task obligations. There is often no one willing, or able, to take over her work. A woman in Koo's study of the health of Regionville described her situation as follows:

> I wish I really knew what you meant about being sick. Sometimes I felt so bad I could curl up and die, but had to go on because the kids had to be taken care of and besides, we didn't have the money to spend for the doctor. How could I be sick? How do you know when you are sick, anyway? Some people can go to bed most anytime with anything, but most of us can't be sick even when we need to be (1954:1).

The third and fourth aspects of the sick role require that patients seek technically competent help and want to get well. The problem with this is that women (who are more often patients) are required to pay to go to male middle-class doctors for their symptoms to receive legitimation as sickness (Lorber, 1975). Thus, they are expected to accept the male definition of their experience and believe that it can be categorized rightly as "depression" or "menopause", for instance. There is another difficulty, too. Women are expected to suffer from psychogenic illness but yet they are required, says Parsons (1951), to want to get better. This is a double bind because psychogenic diseases are said to result from the _desire_ to be ill.

It is clear that Parsons' theory ignores some differences between men and women. Extrapolating from this, it can be seen that the theory ignores all manner of crucial demographic differences such as class, race, ethnicity, sexual preference, and age which serve to repudiate, to various extents, the value of his construct.

Activism

The essence of the activist paradigm is the radical approach to social change. Change is ubiquitous: it is an historical, present, and future reality. The history of all societies is seen as the history of exploitation. Its temporary resolution through the adoption of a new economic system is followed by another, different, exploitive system. Injustice with an ethnic, racial, economic, sexual base has been the inevitable and true historical fact.

Classic radical statements of women and illness are made by Barbara Ehrenreich and Deidre English (1973a, 1973b, 1978). They argue that the medical system is strategic to women's oppression. "Medicine's prime contribution to sexist ideology has been to describe women as sick, and as potentially sickening to men" (1973b: 5). The bio-medical model of the contemporary health-care system reinforces fundamental inequality and injustice in society. They state that women of different economic positions and racial and ethnic backgrounds were not equally and similarly oppressed by the medical care system. The historical distinctions in the causes and kinds of illness which befell women of the working class and middle classes were each described. Class determined the medical categorization, diagnosis, prognosis, and treatment. Upper-class women lived lives of ease and leisure. Working-class women lived lives full of heavy, dirty, and hard work. Upper-class women were viewed as naturally, inherently ill. Believed too delicate for work, emotionally labile, physically fragile, upper class women were the major consumers of the services provided by the physicians of the nineteenth century. Ehrenreich and English argue that this idle, sickly woman was ultimately a product of the economic system. She was an ornament designed to decorate and announce her husband's successful affluence by her leisured indolence. It was considered absolutely appropriate that a woman of this class would break down under such stress as a quarrel with a servant, or a falling out with a girl-friend. Indeed, all _female_ functions and organs were believed to be inherently sick but the root cause of all sickness was an inadequacy in the reproductive system. The theoretical explanation for the frailty of women was the principle of the "conservation of energy," which asserted that each human body had a given quantity of energy to be used. Since a woman's purpose was procreation, the reproductive organs were cherished and rested for their proper function. The obvious conclusion was that higher education or outside careers were not advisable for middle and upper class women.

Lower-class women were thought distinctly different both biologically and socially. Working-class women were strong and immune to disease. They had to work. Employers did not give time off for pregnancy or recovery from childbirth or menstruation. The wives of these same employers often retired to bed on all these occasions (1973b: 47). Working conditions were atrocious. Shops were filthy and ill-kempt, in dangerous irrepair, devoid of sanitation--with the minimum of light and fresh air--and infested with vermin. These women worked ten or more hours a day only to return home to housework, childcare, and "wifeing" in crowded tenements. Likened to oxen or other sturdy animals, they were considered the unhealthy carriers of dangerous and contagious diseases.

These authors further a feminist analysis because they illustrate the manner in which the very conceptions of women of different social classes and racial and ethnic backgrounds embody sexist medicalizing. In doing so, they infer that change is not only a possible but a necessary fact of social life. What this paradigm tends to neglect is the analysis of a situation from the perspective of the subject of study.

Naturalism

The commitment of the naturalist sociologist is to portray the meaning of the social world from the perspective of the subjects of study. The three premises of symbolic interaction are that:

> Human beings act toward things on the basis of the meaning that things have for them; meanings are derived from, or arise out of social interactions that one has with one's fellows; these meanings are handled in and modified through an interpretive process used by the person in dealing with the things he encounters (Blumer, 1969: 2).

"Some Social Meanings of Tranquillizer Use" by Ruth Cooperstock and Henry L. Lennard (1979), illustrates this approach. Positivist sociologists know that minor tranquillizers, especially the benzodiazepines, have become accepted as the appropriate remedy for a variety of types of problems of living, both by physicians and by the population at large (Dunnell and Cartwright, 1972). A number of studies have shown that prescribing psychotropic drugs is not random--but that women, older women in particular--are more than likely the recipients (Cooperstock and Lennard, 1979).

The naturalist's concern, however, is the context in which the tranquillizer use comes to be meaningful to both users and prescribers. Data for this study were gathered through 14 group interviews with 68 participants and 24 lengthy letters from individuals who could not participate. Major themes emerged and were repeated in the group discussions. Tranquillizers were used by women to enable them to handle difficult marriages; to continue in the nurturing role which they believed they ought to perform; or to handle anger and resentment directed at a spouse which they felt powerless to express more directly. Since the advantage of this perspective is that the data are themselves presented, they can speak for themselves. Thus, one women explains:

> I take it to protect the family from my irritability because the kids are kids. I don't think it's fair for me to start yelling at them because their normal activity is bothering me (p. 336).

Role conflict was sometimes the explanation for the use of tranquillizers:

> I would like to be off in Australia somewhere, writing, you know, do only my work. But having to stop the writing to get supper on, it irritates me. And there are so many irritations during the day but

I cannot change the situation because of my family
(p. 337).

Many women reported beginning to use mood-altering drugs when their children were born. Almost consistently, when women returned to work their tranquillizer use diminished or terminated.

And then I realized that I'd better get some of this pressure off at some point. I was afraid I was going to kill my kids...(p. 338).
It turned out we couldn't have children so we adopted ... And with the adoption of the first child, I was deliriously happy ... And then I adopted a second child very quickly after the first, and she was a holy terror. She screamed from the moment we brought her into the house and she never stopped screaming (p. 339).

Sudden personal loss and the strains of adapting to a new role initiated tranquillizer use for many. Unresolved conflicts necessitate continuing use. Males in the sample tended to speak of their tranquillizer use with respect to the strains and stresses of their occupational roles. A minister found his symptoms arose when he changed jobs.

I changed jobs about five years ago from a preaching... job to a human relations job. It's competitive stuff. And about six months later, I started having some ... psychosomatic induced dizziness, a sense of you're about to pass out (p. 340).

As the authors point out, this approach to the study of tranquillizers makes it patently obvious that the biomedical explanation of use is in itself inadequate. Through a refocus in methodology away from the quantitative, naturalist sociology is pertinent to a new model of sociology in which women are not made the object of a study but the subjects in the sociological art of knowing (Smith, 1976). What this paradigm tends to ignore is the social structural aspects of meaningful social life.

Discussion and Conclusion

This chapter describes and illustrates the fundamentals of a multi-paradigmatic approach to sociology with reference to medical sociology. The three paradigms are distinct in their fundamental views of the nature of social reality and in their decision as to the proper methods and theories. There is a long tradition in the sociological literature dating back to Durkheim, Marx, and Weber for these three major paradigms; positivism, activism, and naturalism. Each is appropriate for somewhat different questions, methods, and levels of reality. Together they comprise a more complete, complex, and thorough explanation of the social world.

More specifically this chapter describes the image of women, and the methods and theories for studying them in the context of health care, in each of the three paradigms. To this end, a prototypical manuscript from each of the three paradigms is described and critiqued. Some advantages and disadvantages of each are established.

Each model has strengths and weaknesses. Through positivism, a systems level of discussion with a clarification of causal processes is possible. Evidently positivism, as described, suffers from inadequate attention to sex, sexual preference, class, ethnicity, and race as either explanatory or dependent variables. Activism provides a critical and radical examination of the social action of individuals, groups, and societies. It assumes injustice and exploitation. It neglects to explore the personal meanings of injustice, however, and attempts to designate those men and women who do not recognize their exploitation or exploitedness as suffering from false consciousness. The naturalist perspective provides, in rich and intimate language, the details of the experience of women. It tends to neglect, however, the provision of an adequate conceptual or methodological recognition of the existence of a level of social reality before and above the individual social actor.

To thoroughly incorporate the principles of feminist analysis (described by Millman and Kanter, 1975; Roberts, 1981b; Smith, 1976), all three paradigms are necessary. They interweave to form a variegated mesh which is more complete because it is more multi-faceted. Medical sociology has been dominated by a positivist approach. This has meant that the emphasis has been placed on the existing society and has taken for granted the structures and values of the existing society. It also has meant that outside attempts at an objective analysis have been stressed at the expense of the subjective meaning to the social actors; that private worlds have been neglected in favour of public worlds; that the potential for a radically altered future has been dismissed in the face of the overwhelming reality of the present; that formal arrangements and structures have been described with the loss of the informal; that male language, models and methods have been utilized to the detriment of women and that sex, race, ethnicity, class, and sexual preference have not often been taken into account as factors in behaviour--even though they may be among the most important explanatory variables.

A second drawback of a reliance on positivism is methodological myopism. Numerous studies have documented the need for a multi-methods approach in sociology. As Denzin says, "No single method is uniformly superior; each has its own special strengths and weaknesses. It is time for sociologists to recognize this fact and to move on to a position that permits them to approach their problems with all relevant and appropriate methods, to move on to the strategy of methodological triangulation (1978:339)." Methodological triangulation can take many forms. A combination of multiple data collection methods, multiple data types, analytic styles, observers and theories in the same investigation is advocated. Thus, social reality is approached from numerous vantage points in respect to both theory and method.

A sociology of medicine that begins by (1) noting, describing, analysing and questioning the existing structures which perpetuate this sexism and (2) acknowledging the importance of women's experience will go a long way in correcting it. These two conditions may be met by a dynamic, dialectic use of multi-methods and multi-theories addressed to an exploration and explanation of the same problem. A conscientious effort at triangulation could be useful in several ways. Observing, describing, analysing and challenging the taken-for-granted structure may lead to the improvement of existing conditions for women both in the world and in the substantive discipline of the sociology of medicine.

Lesbianism, Feminism, and Social Science

Vera Whisman

The relationship between lesbianism and feminism has not been an easy one. The lesbian presence in the women's movement has sometimes been a source of curiosity, fear and resentment from heterosexual feminists. Nonetheless, it is largely through feminism that lesbians have found a voice, as many lesbians come to feel more closely tied to straight women than to gay men.

This shift of allegiance has had scholarly and theoretical results, none so important as the attempt to redefine lesbianism in feminist terms. The definition of lesbianism as a personal matter of sexual preference has been abandoned in favor of a definition of lesbianism as political. First articulated by Simone de Beauvoir, and propounded in the Radicalesbians' well known "Woman-Identified Woman" paper (1972), the idea was expanded and explored by Adrienne Rich (1980; see also Myron and Bunch, 1975).

Briefly, the lesbian-feminist argument is that lesbianism is, at some level (whether intentionally or implicitly), an act of rebellion against male supremacy, one beachhead of which is institutionalized heterosexuality. These writers hold that this is what lesbianism *is*; there may be a sexual component, but it is neither necessary nor the essence of lesbianism.

Disagreement about lesbian-feminism and related topics, such as anti-pornography feminism, has come to be called the "sex debate." I hope to show that the very real, political problems that lesbian and feminist ideas and definitions share are expressions of difficulties that sociologists also face. That is, they are problems rooted deeply in the attempt to analyze social experience.

The Sociology of Deviance

Lesbianism has long been considered--in the public as well as the academic mind--a form of deviance. It, after all, breaks a well-established norm--that of heterosexuality. But in sociology, this sort of approach to deviance has largely been replaced by the labeling approach. Labeling theory's fundamental insight is that nothing is inherently deviant. And while a large body of work within the theory has concentrated on the consequences of the labeling process for per_sons_, another has branched off to consider why and how certain types of behav_ior_ have come to be labeled "deviant."

This broader approach to labeling theory shares with political lesbianism a concern for uncovering the source of the broadly accepted definition of lesbianism as deviant sexuality. This concern involves the question, "Whose definition is it?", the answer to which must consider power.

Working toward a "politics-of-labeling" perspective, Lauderdale (1976) showed that the creation of a deviance category is a "movement of moral boundaries." That is, the same behavior may be at one time included in the lexicon of "normal" behaviors, and at another be categorized as deviant, as the boundaries between categories themselves shift. He also illustrates how this shift may be a response to a perceived threat, either from outside the social system or from within, as a "realignment of power."

From here it is possible to conceive of the redefinition of lesbianism as an attempt, in this case by the "deviants" themselves, to redraw boundaries. Further, if lesbianism is in some way an act of rebellion, recognition of that by the dominants would certainly be perceived as a threat, a possible "realignment of power."

Lesbian-feminists, by viewing lesbianism as rebellion, are engaged in what Schur (1980) calls "a struggle over competing definitions" with those who consider lesbianism as a personal, sexual choice. Interestingly, the struggle is taking place within the women's movement, and not in the "public forum."[1] Nevertheless, since the movement itself may be seen as a social system where some have more power than others, the concept of power struggle is applicable.

Here, then, is the outline of a perspective which is shared by the sociology of deviance and political lesbianism: Deviance is that behavior which is so defined by those who have the power to make such a definition and to give it consequence. The reason they label something "deviant" includes the perception that the behavior (or the "deviant" herself) constitutes a threat. Finally, the "deviants" do not necessarily accept their stigmatization, and may fight it by collectively redefining what they "do."

Political Lesbianism

The idea that lesbianism is rebellion, that it is an implicitly political act and can (or should) be an explicitly political act is often expressed or assumed in the letters and articles of lesbian-feminist periodicals. Some of these letters are from women who have themselves chosen lesbianism for explicitly political, feminist reasons. If the redefinition of lesbianism referred only to these "new lesbians," it would inspire little argument. Stating that feminists who become lesbians for political reasons are involved in a political act is not a redefinition at all, but is simply naming a new behavior. The redefinition of lesbianism seeks to connect the experience of these women with that of other women who are neither feminist nor lesbian.

Lillian Faderman (1981) attempts to make that connection historically. She documents the widespread existence from the 16th to the 19th century of exclusive, romantic relationships between women; "romantic friendships." As women were not considered sexual creatures, these relationships were not thought to be sexual and because the relationships did not replace heterosexual marriage, they were not seen as threatening, or even odd.

The era of an open, "normal," love between women came to an end at the turn of the 20th century, when social and economic changes allowed a few women to support themselves and, if they chose, to substitute a female lover for a husband. This fact, set against the backdrop of a growing women's movement, disturbed and threatened men.

In the same period, the early sexologists--Freud, Ellis and Kraft-Ebbing--discovered not only that women could be sexual, but that they could be sexual with each other. One effect of the wide diffusion of information on "clinical lesbianism" was that relationships between women became--by definition and in practice--sexual. Another was that those who benefitted from male domination now had a weapon to use against that which threatened them. That weapon was a new deviance category.

Faderman's perspective is compatible with a "politics of labeling" approach, as she emphasizes threat, the "movement of moral boundaries," and the notion that deviance labels are the tools of a power struggle. If a politics-of-labeling sociology is her perspective, then political lesbianism is her theme, for the notion that relationships between women are a rebellion is implicit in her work. In a world where women are to belong to men, "'Lesbian' describes a relationship in which two women's strongest emotions and affections are directed toward each other" (Faderman, 1981: 17).

The attempt to find continuity between past and present relationships between women requires downplaying the sexual, as lesbian sexuality seems to be a recent historical phenomenon. Adrienne Rich (1980) locates lesbian sexuality on a "lesbian continuum," defined to include "a range...of woman-identified experience; not simply the fact that a woman has had or consciously desired genital sexual experience with another woman" (Rich, 1980:638).

Rich's argument, briefly, is this: Heterosexuality, institutionalized and strongly enforced, is an integral part of the oppression of women. As such, refusing heterosexuality is a rebellion against one aspect of male supremacy. This refusal may take many forms--20th century lesbian sexuality and African secret women's societies, to name two--all of which fall somewhere on Rich's "lesbian continuum."

These works on the redefinition of lesbianism are related to a sociology of deviance in two ways. First, they fall _within_ the sociology of deviance, analyzing, with Schur and others, the politics of deviance-defining. Secondly, the redefinition of lesbianism is also a subject of study _by_ the sociology of deviance. It is in itself a part of a power struggle, as it is used to shape feminist goals and strategies. So the redefinition of lesbianism has a dual nature: It is at the same time an _analysis_ of lesbianism, its stigmatization and its place in women's struggle against oppression, and it is a _tool_ for use in that struggle.

Critiques of Political Lesbianism

The major criticism of the redefinition of lesbianism is that the concept is ahistorical: Lesbian sexuality is a recent phenomenon, and its emergence resulted in the creation of a lesbian _identity_ which previously did not exist. Lesbians now--as opposed to "romantic friends" then--think of themselves as lesbians. The behavior of these two groups, however similar, carries very different meanings for the actors, and so there is no continuity, but rather a sharp distinction.

A second, and related, criticism is directed at the redefinition of lesbianism as ideology and states that de-emphasizing sexuality may be more than an attempt to gloss over historical differences; it may also reflect an anti-sex bias, a consistent underestimation of the importance of sexual pleasure (Zita, 1981). This charge often comes from "butch" and "femme" lesbians,[2] whose lifestyles are often dismissed by lesbian-feminists as "coming out of the past oppression of lesbians who had no other models" (Myron and Bunch, 1975). These "old style" lesbians explain that the roles of butch and femme are about sex, about "what lesbians do." A butch appearance is a symbol of meaning, not that a woman is mannish, but that she is sexually aggressive with other women. If political lesbians are "embarrassed" by butch/femmes perhaps it is because they are also embarassed by sexuality (Nestle, 1981; Califia, 1980).

Lesbian sadomasochists have also been hard hit by the redefinition of lesbianism, and here again their behavior is interpreted as a reflection of patriarchal relations between men and women. The Coalition for a Feminist Sexuality and Against Sadomasochism distributed a flyer at the Barnard College Conference on Sexuality that read in part:

> This coalition is not criticizing any woman for having internalized sex roles or for having sadomasochistic fantasies...But (S/M lesbians) are

not acknowledging having internalized patriarchal messages and values.

The interesting contradiction here is that this flyer echoes the dominant attitude toward lesbians: "They can't help it, but they ought not to promote it either." Again, lesbian-feminism seems anti-sex (Califia, 1981).

Some have argued that the redefinition of lesbianism reflects as anti-sex bias by pointing to its class origins. The proponents of the redefinition are mostly white middle-class women, whereas black women in general and working class white women are more likely to be involved in butch/femme relationships (Nestle, 1981). Thus, the redefinition of lesbianism may be a reflection of white middle-class repressive sexuality.

A third criticism of the redefinition of lesbianism is that, as an ideological tool, it is elitist. If lesbianism is inherently political, then those lesbians who experience it as a mainly sexual activity are somehow less than "real lesbians" (Zita, 1981). The very idea of a continuum invites this criticism, as one suspects that the "most lesbian" end of Rich's continuum is occupied by that recently evolved group of women whose lesbianism is consciously political.

A related criticism comes from heterosexual feminists. Their anger at being defined as "traitors" is well expressed in a letter to WIRES:

(This is) the first time I've seen feminists directly deny the principle that every woman's experience is real and valid (Leeds Revolutionary Feminist Group, 1981, p. 11)

Taken together, the criticisms show that the redefinition of lesbianism is a weak analytical concept because it is ahistorical; it glosses over too many real differences, especially lesbian sexuality and experience. As an ideological tool, it is elitist, dividing women into the "politically correct and incorrect" based on their sexuality.

Political Lesbianism and Feminism

It is difficult to name any central tenet of feminist theory. If there is a commonality, it is perhaps the basic concept that the "personal is political." To make that point, feminists have made connections between social phenomena that have been considered unrelated. Making these connections often involves redefining a concept in new terms, a method frequently used by feminists to reveal the political nature of women's experience. Recently this method has been used to analyze and act against pornography.

In a feminist vocabulary, the term "pornography" means sexual material whose message "is violence, dominance and conquest" (Steinem, 1980). But in what way do representations of degradation and violence actually demean and hurt women?[3] Evidence about connections between individual's use of pornography and practice of rape is not conclusive. But when Robin Morgan (1980) states that "pornography is the theory and rape is the practice," she refers not to an individual cause and effect relationship, but to pornography's function as propaganda for sexism.

Like political feminism, antipornography feminism is seen as anti-sex. Critics point out that much of what feminists consider pornographic does not really demean women--for example the image of the dominatrix (Alderfer, et al., 1982). And pornography seems to send a dual message: the one the antipornography feminists emphasize, and one that says that women can enjoy and seek out sexual pleasure and be "bad girls." To those who emphasize the latter, antipornography feminists seem like a "bunch of good girls on a rampage" (Orlando, 1982).

Others ask why, out of all the propaganda for misogyny, the explicitly sexual has been singled out for attention. Gothic novels, for example, are also rooted in violence against women and a "rape mentality," but because they represent a _repressed_ sexuality, they are not a subject of concern for antipornography feminists (Willis, 1981).

As in the critiques of lesbian-feminism, the criticisms of anti-sex bias and elitism are related. "Correct and incorrect" reactions to pornography have emerged:

> One recollection of the WAP (Women Against Pornography) tour is that viewers were supposed to be disgusted by the slides. One woman said some material turned her on; others greeted her remark with shock and denial (Alderfer, et al., 1982: 17).

Just as the redefinition of lesbianism is ahistorical, placing different experiences in the same category, so antipornography feminism is "at the point of complete conflation of sex and violence" (Alderfer, et al. 1982). It also cannot decisively distinguish between pornography and erotica (Orlando, 1982).

Feminism and Social Theory

I have tried to show, through the critique of political lesbianism and antipornography feminism, that these two feminist analyses are very similar in their use of a logic that is common in feminist writing. I suggest that the problems of feminist theory are problems of social theory in general. For, as political lesbianism uses the analytical concepts of deviance sociology, so general feminism also uses social science concepts. The charge that feminist theory carries an anti-sex bias also seems valid, and I suspect that this is largely due to the class background of most of the theorists. But even so, there are many class-specific biases in feminism; why has sex emerged as a line of division? The reasons must surely include our culture's ambivalent attitudes about sex. Largely because of this, sex is an area that is particularly vulnerable to a non-interpretive analysis--analysis which ignores the meaning that people's behavior has _for them_. If a topic is not handled openly and supportively, then how easy it is to say "This is what you are feeling." The anti-sex bias in feminist theory, then, is related to--but not reduceable to--its noninterpretive stance.

The place of interpretation has long been a problem for social scientists. At one extreme is the explanatory approach, which often uses terms such as "false consciousness" for individuals' interpretations of their own behavior. Listen to Adrienne Rich and Emile Durkheim:

> The issue of "lesbian sadomasochism" needs to be examined in terms of the dominant culture's teachings (Rich, 1980)

> Human deliberations...so far as reflective consciousness affects them are often only purely formal (Durkheim, 1951)

That is, people do not know what they are doing, or why they are doing it.

At the other extreme is a hesitancy to ever say that two actions are "the same kind of thing," a belief that "understanding must necessarily presuppose...the participant's unreflective understanding" (Winch, 1977: 148). Ferguson agrees with Winch when she criticizes Rich for including women in a category they would not comprehend. The interpretive approach, however, can be so radical that there is no room for analysis at all, for setting up any categories other than those which people already understand through their experience. And these categories are strongly influenced by the dominant ideology.

Feminism offers us a chance to see what happens when social theories become ideologies. The search for causal explanations in analysis becomes elitism in political practice, and analysis based solely on interpretation is not political at all. At the explanatory extreme, lesbianism is defined as political, and those who experience it differently are left out. At the interpretive extreme lesbianism is, perhaps, whatever a lesbian makes of it, and has no political significance at all. Feminism is divided by a dispute that, on the surface, is about sex. Beneath that surface simmers a conflict between causal explanation and interpretation. If so, then the answer is not to continue fighting about sex, and perfecting already established arguments, but to begin to understand, on a deeper level, the origins of the "feminist sex debate."

NOTES

[1] What does appear in the public debate is a conflict over whether lesbianism is a pathological sexuality or a normal lifestyle choice. This is a struggle to destigmatize lesbianism using the terms in which it is already defined. The political lesbianism argument goes farther.

[2] Butch/femme relationships are those in which the two women take on distinct roles--one ostensibly masculine, the other appearing feminine.

[3] Aside from the models and actresses used in its production. The essence of the theory is that pornography hurts *all* women.

Feminism and Sociology:
An Unfortunate Case of Nonreciprocity

Mary White Stewart

Reflexive Statement

Throughout the past ten years, as my identity both as a sociologist and a feminist has emerged, each has been consistent with the other. Yet, though I relied heavily on sociological analyses and interpretations in the development of my feminist perspective, sociology as a discipline seemed to remain detached from and relatively uninformed by feminism. It appeared that this same lack of mutuality occurred in other areas which provided vigor and excitement to the development of feminist thought but which were not in turn similarly benefited. This paper grew from my efforts to understand how a field which had so strongly nurtured my feminism could remain so unaffected by a perspective which it helped to engender.

Feminism and Sociology

Feminist scholarship has grown dramatically since the reemergence of the women's movement in the early 1960's. It has, in fact, merged with feminist action to broaden and strengthen the women's movement. Feminist scholarship is part of a movement which has radically altered our social world, a movement which William Chafe (1972) claims has altered our consciousness and our institutions more than any other movement of this century. Among the most active feminist scholars are sociologists, women who for the most part did not gain feminist consciousness until after graduate school. There were precious few women in the Ph.D. programs in the sixties and they were learning a male sociology from male professors in a patriarchal institution. They were viewed and often viewed themselves as fortunate to be able to think like men while being blessed with feminine attributes, and women were reluctant to confront these evaluations. They learned their sociology well, traditional sociology as well as radical sociology, and they were later able to put their knowledge to use building feminist scholarship.

As the women's movement emerged out of the anti-war movement, the civil rights movement and dramatic changes in social and economic conditions, some sociologists developed a feminist perspective and began to name themselves feminists. The women's movement was not initially taken seriously by most sociologists--men saw it as peripheral and were reluctant to respond to the feminist challenge. Some women academics feared loss of professional respect if they became too closely aligned with feminism. Others felt isolated and ineffectual in offering what became predictable challenges to the male-defined and male-dominated system in which they worked. Many women who finished graduate school in or before the early seventies had developed little feminist consciousness in their professionalization process and hence offered no challenge to the dominant sociological interpretations which viewed women as of interest only in their deviations from the roles of mother and wife; that is to say, as a primary, and potentially destructive, socializing agent. Thus, feminist sociologists had a niche between a potentially supportive profession with embedded patriarchal knowledge and assumptions that structurally limited the practice and knowledge of the discipline.

The specialty areas within sociology of obvious relevance to the development of feminist thought and analysis are family, deviance, stratification, and organization. These areas, while providing useful information and perspectives to feminists, paid little specific attention to women's realities or discussed them in a pattern of stereotypes which diminished their potential applicability. Feminist sociologists working in these areas drew from them the rich detail which would provide the groundwork for their analysis, an analysis forged from the many questions feminists raised which were unanswered (often unasked) by traditional sociology.

Once women began to move beyond the limits which accompanied male-defined sociology, the questions they posed focused not only on women's lives and how they differed from men's but also on the underlying "taken for granted" world of male sociologists.

Once women began to ask themselves the simple question which Adrienne Rich had posed, "What is life like for women?", they became increasingly aware of the power of their own field to provide answers, and the answers led to increasingly complex questions. Feminist consciousness led to the unavoidable conclusion that this crucial question was seen as both irrelevant and unimportant, and that for sociologists women were essentially invisible.

Feminists with their theoretical perspective and analytical skills found that sociology offered an abundance of material for the development of feminist analysis. They gleaned from their field what it had to offer, reanalyzing, reinterpreting, reformulating, digging under the heavy patriarchal bias to discover and create. They joined with feminist scholars in other disciplines who were engaged in the same process of questioning and discovering. We now turn to a consideration of the tie between feminist sociology and various dominant theoretical perspectives.

Feminist Sociologists and Symbolic Interactionism

Once women began the process of making women visible, there were a number of ways in which established, patriarchal sociology nurtured feminist sociology and supported the growth of the women's movement, albeit unwittingly. Sociology provided a wealth of theoretical and conceptual resources on many levels from the structural to the interactionist. Very clearly, the symbolic interactionists' conceptualization of social reality provided in the work of such authors as Berger and Luckmann (1967), Becker (1963), Goffman (1963) and Garfinkle (1967) offered a strong base from which feminists could develop a new reality system and challenge the old. Feminists who bridled under the definition of women as inadequate, weak and castrating, and who condemned the restrictions and traps of the role of mother and wife in our culture (Rich, 1976; Daly, 1978; Chesler, 1972) and who were criticized as placing too much importance on words could gain support from sociological perspectives which saw symbols as the building blocks of our culture, the actual reality upon which the more visible rules and regulations were built. As Garfinkle (1967) suggested, the everyday "taken for granted" reality, that which was so subtle as not to be differentiated or visible to us, was *the* significant social fabric.

The symbolic interactionist perspective furthermore provided support to feminists who condemned the image of women in advertising and the media. The dichotomous definitions of woman as sexually anesthetized or sexually crazed, as a madonna or a bitter barren bitch, as castrator or smotherer, were images available in abundance, and readily provided by writers from Sigmund Freud (1974) to Nancy Friday (1977). Feminists who did not find mother-in-law jokes funny and who did not laugh at the derision of older women or applaud the winners of the Miss or Mrs. America contests, feminists who were furious about the explanations for wife battering, rape and incest that subtly or blatantly implicated the victim found support among sociologists who saw jokes, everyday language and expert explanations as creations, not merely reflections, of reality.

It was clear to feminist sociologists as well as historians, psychologists and other academicians that what had been presented as truth was simply one reality system. The social creationists provided theoretical support for the assertion that the traditional truths excluded women and did not represent their reality.

Socially established truth, although certainly not fragile, could be seen as permeable--as vulnerable to change. If damaging and degrading myths about women were a male-created "truth," then evidence of this could be ferreted out of history books, could be dredged from the primordial mud and examined as a set of social artifacts. History did not carry the heavy weight of truth but instead was seen as a selective presentation of information reflecting the values and biases of not only the male historians but also the male-oriented culture in which they wrote.

But the obvious questions of vested interest and power in the creation of a culture which defined women to their detriment were not posed by most symbolic interactionists. Rather, the conflict theorists were far more likely to offer an applicable analysis of power. Until the recent work of Scott (1969), Pfohl (1977), Conrad and Schneider (1980), and Spector and Kitsuse (1979) the discussion of power (which is so obviously suggested by any orientation that suggests truth is a social creation) is too often side-stepped by the interactionists. This perspective--which had been so compatible with the feminist pursuit of redefining woman and her future and which described reality and culture as an ongoing, not totally self-conscious, creation of active agents in the world--offered little that was concrete to feminists who were unraveling the threads of power and privilege in the political and economic institutions of this country. Perhaps the flaws discovered by feminists when analyzing women's reality were the same flaws that prevented symbolic interactionism from becoming a more powerful component of sociology in the first place.

Feminist Sociology and Theories of Oppression

Early in the academic feminist literature on women's oppression, images of class and conflict were evoked, and parallels were drawn between women and blacks. Hacker (1951) wrote on the similarities of women and blacks as oppressed minority groups, de Beauvoir (1953) established a Marxist analysis as the appropriate one for female oppression and anthropologists drew a convincing picture of cross-cultural oppression of women. Many feminist writers, using the terms "class" and "minority groups" more or less loosely, spoke and perceived of women as an oppressed or disadvantaged class. There were however, many disagreements as to the appropriateness and accuracy of a traditional class analysis. The question of accuracy and the criticism of Marxism for inadequately explaining women's oppression in the family and not distinguishing between male and female same-class oppression were in some cases of secondary significance to the perceived political and moral appropriateness of such an analysis. The relationship between academic scholarship and the active women's movement influenced the acceptance of race and class analyses. Despite this appearance of compatibility, white guilt was strong, and the black power movement was protective of its turf. The similarity between the black power movement and the women's movement and between the oppression of blacks and women might be easily drawn theoretically, but in actual practice middle class white women knew that a sense of themselves as distant cousins seemed more realistic than their being embraced as a group of sisters. Class analysis might enhance understanding of women's oppression, but the black power movement and the women's movement were more often at odds than walking arm in arm. The same was true for much of the New Left and the women's movement, especially that portion which had emerged and gained consciousness in the New Left.

Grappling with issues of class oppression was difficult not only because of obvious theoretical complexities but also because living a life consistent with the analysis created its own complexities. Women were often criticized for living with the oppressor if they were married, or as male-identified if they related to males, yet faced the likelihood of sinking into poverty if they did not. Heterosexual women faced the common assertion that the only politically correct choice was to become a lesbian, a choice that offended both lesbians who felt ripped off by so-called political lesbians and those straight women who intended to remain so. The rhetoric was in many cases a bit less confusing than the actual practice of establishing life on an on-going basis that felt right for the participants. The painful, challenging, controversial and often agonizing conclusion drawn by a large segment of the feminist population that "the personal is political" was a statement of the deep, intricate ties between the self and the social system. Women's experience was a reflection of their mutual conditions, conditions which the feminist activists were devoted to changing.

Feminist Sociology and Functionalism

Functionalist sociologists, despite their academic interest in questions of structure, power, bureaucracy and organization, offered feminists a good foil. Functionalism, a perspective focusing on the intricate yet happy marriage of various units in a society for the maintenance of social equilibrium, has long been one of the most persuasive and powerful perspectives in sociology. Because it views stasis and value consensus as normal, and upheaval and dissensus as abnormal and temporary, it is unlikely that functionalists would accurately assess the importance and long term significance of the implications of the women's movement.

Yet functionalist analyses of women's place in marriage, family and the world at large and the acceptance and incorporation of such analyses by so many sociologists led to reanalyses and powerful feminist criticism. Although clearly the various units could peacefully function as Parsons suggested, any consideration of the oppression of women resulting from such a well-oiled machine was missing. Once again women could see how academic truisms were not benign assumptions, but political statements actively supporting a world view damaging to women. It may have seemed less possible to restructure sociology, so much of which was built upon misunderstanding or ignorance of women's lives, than it was to join other feminists in a new feminist analysis. Although they did not abandon sociology or sociological analysis, many feminists began to move away emotionally and intellectually.

Feminist Sociology as a Critique of Sociological Practice

Feminism, with its challenge to traditional, individualistic, oppressive definitions of women, opened the door for contributions by sociologists, contributions which would have received public consideration as a result of the newsworthy nature of the women's movement. But although feminist sociologists have made significant contributions to understanding the lives of women, sociology as a field has not provided a credible alternative to the individualistic explanations for behavior which are so deeply engrained in our cultures. In fact, Szasz (1966, 1976) and Scheff (1976), psychiatric insiders, have gained far more attention for their challenges to the individualistic model than have sociologists, the obvious critics. The clear, precise, thought-provoking works of such authors as Conrad and Schneider (1980) and Spector and Kitsuse (1979), I suggest, are simply accepted as interesting, esoteric interpretations of something "we all know about" rather than as deep criticisms of the familiar world. Indeed, these authors built on a long history of challenges to individualistic explanations -- C.W. Mills (1943) condemned what he called the "social work" ideology and its spread to all human problems. The concern of those who challenge the individualistic perspective is at least partially a response to its strength and pervasiveness. Psychologists and psychiatrists, based on their professional training, create individualistic explanations for human behavior. These explanations are legitimated and codified easily, being consistent with legal ideologies. They are disseminated to the general public who express enlightenment by seeking therapeutic intervention when they are in trouble--intervention which then predictably focuses on individual characteristics or problems. This is not a conspiracy. This is the result of the involvement of an increasing number of trained persons actively engaged in an enterprise which is saleable, actively searching for new territories, audiences, problems and interpretations.

If the perspectives offered by sociologists and feminists, perspectives which are compatible and potentially mutually reinforcing, are to gain power and actually effect social change, public conceptions of the nature of reality must change. Feminism has surely had a more significant and broader impact on these public conceptions than has sociology. Sociology as a profession has been self-consciously, timidly restrained, throwing occasional ineffectual darts from the sideline, yet missing the opportunity to make policy statements and to be effective in the world. Sociology as a profession has not comfortably embraced feminist belief systems, nor for that matter any potentially political belief system, since the sixties. This is largely due to the fact that feminist ideology challenges so much of what is inherently a male model of social structure and reality. A feminist consciousness demands that the old visions be changed and leads to a sensitization to issues and ideas which create unpheavals in the established system of thought. Some of the less obvious reasons for the limited impact of the sociological perspective are the failure of will on the part of academic sociologists, the hesitation to approach a subject with gusto, the fear of investing the self in the activity and the defensive employment of concepts and theories which are unattached to the complex reality which includes women.

The Feminist Agenda

Feminist sociologists, as Anderson (1983) points out, have vigorously embraced the promise of their discipline. Sociology originally was devoted to the ideal of social progress, to the application of the scientific method, to the improvement of life for humankind, and feminists accepted that goal. Furthermore, feminists are good empiricists, recognizing that when theory is inconsistent with experience, the theory needs to be revised or rejected.

Feminists embraced their subject with gusto, vigorously participating in the creative process of building. Mainstream sociologists maintained a defensive posture, incorporating feminist insight only peripherally and only when doing so called for no restructuring of basic theoretical assumptions. Sociology had so completely ignored women or had, in other cases, included them so narrowly, that to actually incorporate feminist sociological analysis would have require significant, deep restructuring of sociological thought. It sometimes proved easier to (and far more stimulating) for feminist sociologists to share their analyses with other feminist scholars than to talk with sociologists. Surely they did not simply reject their disciplines--in some cases the battles to change them were long and hard as in the case of the Modern Language Association's strife over the significance and meaning of pronouns. Sometimes they created caucuses or interest groups in their own discipline, such as Sociologists for Women in Society, but they also aligned themselves creatively with other feminists, establishing organizations such as the National Women's Studies Association. They produced an impressive record of publications, journals, critiques and feminist associations. Journals such as *Signs*, *Trivia*, *Feminist Studies* and *Quest* provided scholarly forums for academic women. Simultaneously an increasing number of feminist articles on women's lives began appearing in such journals as *Journal of Marriage and the Family*, *American Journal of Sociology*, *Journal of Social Issues* and *Social Problems*.

Feminists from all disciplines joined with one another, taking with them the riches of their own fields and creating a new intellectual, political and personal alliance. Women put their ideas before a variety of audiences but seemed less interested in attempts to convince fellow sociologists than to develop their ideas through contact with other feminist scholars. All of this has been beneficial to the development of feminist studies, but sociology as a field has been little enhanced.

While feminist sociologists have actively worked to achieve social change, mainstream sociology on the contrary has been reluctant to participate in changing the society it studies or to apply its findings to activites in the world. Rather than use sociological understanding to improve our social world, or to effect structural and personal change as both the early sociologists and the feminist scholars have done, mainstream sociology finds its usefulness and significance increasingly questionable. Sociology is losing ground in the battle to define social reality, social problems and their solutions to the individualistic disciplines. It has turned away from an active involvement with the hurly burly world which nourished its beginning to an antiseptic affair with the most common symbol of the machine age--the computer and its love offerings: simplicity, speed, elegance and aloofness from the world beyond its terminal. The robust nature of feminist scholarship is drawn from its immersion in the dynamic changes of the economic, political and social world and its self-confidence as an analyst of these changes. Perhaps now it is time for sociology, which has proved to be rich and fertile environment for the development of feminist thought, to incorporate the feminist perspective (which broadens and refreshes sociology by including the reality of women) and a feminist relationship with the world (which is both sensuous and robust) to regain its failing strength and faltering purpose.

Am I My Sister's Gatekeeper?: Cautionary Tales from the Academic Hierarchy

Judith A. Cook and Mary Margaret Fonow

Refelexive Statement

Our collaboration began over a decade ago when, as graduate students, we developed our ideologies as feminists and as sociologists. During these years, we have advised and assisted each other in negotiating many rites of passage, resulting in both personal and professional familiarity with gatekeeping processes. Our critical reflection upon these experiences has strengthened our commitment to feminist approaches in research, and fostered our interest in revealing linkages between the structure of bias in sociology and the production of feminist scholarship.

Introduction

Perhaps the overriding reason the gatekeeping process is so familiar to feminist scholars is that they confront it continually throughout their careers. Working from a feminist perspective generally evokes disapproving or even hostile scrutiny from those individuals who control access to advancement opportunities in academic hierarchies. This is problematic given that professional achievement is fundamentally tied to a scholar's ability to please the relevant gatekeepers she encounters during her career.

In this analysis, we will address the issue of academic gatekeeping and how it influences the nature of feminist scholarship. We have chosen to explore the inter-linkages between academic gatekeeping and the structure of social relations within the discipline of sociology. This has been done in order to understand how the properties of gender asymmetry are incoporated into the analytical and practical procedures of social science.

The fundamental feature of gatekeepers is the power they derive from controlling access to valued resources. One of the most important academic resources monitored by gatekeepers is _publication_ of journal articles, texts, readers, and monographs, since scholarship which is not in print "does not exist" in a professionally legitimated sense (Spender, 1981b: 188). Another type of valued resource concerns _ideas_ _and_ _criteria_; gatekeepers are in a position to decree innovations in thought, techniques and values, to set standards and define accepted viewpoints, and to monitor ontological shifts (Smith, 1976). Finally, gatekeepers control access to the more material rewards of _jobs_ _and_ _money_; hiring and promotion decisions are made by those in power while research funding is dispensed through private and public channels which are safe-guarded by "already-proven" evaluators (Nebraska Sociological Feminist Collective, 1983).

In what follows, we examine the process of gatekeeping as it occurs in four broad contexts for sociologists working in a university setting. These contexts are: 1) selection of research topics and monitoring of ideas and innovations; 2) obtaining funding through the proposal submission process; 3) publishing and the nature of the peer review; and 4) hiring, promotion and tenure processes.

Selection of Topics

The exclusion of the feminist viewpoint and the female world as a focus of inquiry has been linked to three interdependent pre-judgements. The first is the tendency to perceive a topic or area as non-legitimate when it is investigated by a feminist. The second is a tendency to perceive a topic as non-legitimate when it incorporates and focuses on feminist issues. The third consists of a tendency to judge a topic or area as "distorted" or "biased" if it is approached through a feminist mode of presentation and is analyzed reflecting a female world-view.

The refusal to grant importance to topics because they are studied by feminists is related to a penchant for viewing men as authorities. Dorothy Smith refers to this as "a circle effect - men attend to and treat as significant what men say and have said" (1979: 137). Throughout written history, men's activities have been considered relevant to men and have been written "by men about men for men" to create a contemporary discourse which houses "the past within the present" (ibid.).

Because of their dominant role in the creation of knowledge, male social scientists are invested with a "cognitive authority" in which their interpretations of cultural phenomena and their views of social reality are taken as the definitive understandings (Addelson, 1983: 165). One basis of this cognitive authority is the use of rational criticism to examine competing explanations and assumptions. But while rationality is revered in social science, the role of reason in the competition of ideas concerning women has been strangely absent (Epstein, 1981). More often, individual prejudices and preferences serve as the basis for deciding which areas are "worthy" of investigation. As one sociologist describes her decision to postpone research on rape until after she gets tenure, "It is quite clear that doing research on rape is not acceptable...it isn't professional, basically. It is sort of the lowest possible subject you could do anything on, in terms of prestige and status" (M. Thompson, 1983: 74-75). Similarly, a survey of sociology department heads found that one quarter to two-fifths expected campus gatekeepers to disapprove of research on homosexuality (ASA Task Group, 1982). Two additional surveys of sociologists interested in pursuing research on lesbians and gays found that roughly half in each group reported encountering obstacles and receiving discouragement from other colleagues and advisers (1982: 12).

Gatekeepers influence not only the choice of topic but the way in which it is pursued as well. While some may be willing to admit the need for "adding-in" research to areas in which women have previously been ignored (e.g., stratification, mobility, employment), they draw the line when the approach is focused solely on women. There is a tendency to devalue the validity of any type of feminist standpoint or world-view stemming from women's concrete everyday life experiences (Hartsock, 1983). So, for example, a study focusing on businesswomen's workplace relationships with one another was criticized by a reviewer for the journal Sociology of Work and Occupations who asked "How do these women compare with men? How can the findings possibly be interpreted? The research is basically a fishing expedition asking women to say in detail how they relate to other women...one simply cannot make anything of the findings." Clearly, for this gatekeeper the results of a study of woman-to-woman relationship could not be interpreted without reference to men; hence, restriction of the topic to women's experience was not acceptable scholarship.

This attitude that feminist concerns are not a legitimate focus of inquiry stems in part from the "power of naming" which "denies reality and value to that which is never named, never uttered" (DuBois, 1983: 108). The newness of a feminist tradition of sociological research and theory allows gatekeepers to make the assumption that such concerns are not within the mainstream of the discipline and should thus be excluded. Some observers have proposed that as the volume of feminist studies grows larger it will become harder and harder to ignore (Bernard, 1981). While there is no doubt some truth to this argument, it provides little solace to those who are responsible for <u>creating</u> a tradition for which they cannot yet expect to reap full benefits. In fact, this is the dilemma of feminist researchers in sociology: opening up new topics and areas of investigation is a basic feminist goal, yet, the very definition of scholarship within their discipline involves relating their work to a body of literature which often ignores, trivializes or pathologizes women's experiences.

Obtaining Funding

Much less has been written about the effects of gatekeeping on the funding of feminist sociological research, although there appears to be agreement on the fact that funding for feminist studies is harder to obtain (Epstein, 1981). Noting that public and private organizations dispense their money according to topical area, Addelson has pointed out that certain meta-physical and methodological assumptions underlie particular topics (1983). So, for example, a request for proposals to examine the "victim prone personality" traits of battered women is likely to be answered by those researchers whose theoretical approach involves blaming-the-victim for her problems (Pagelow, 1979). Moreover, funding agencies are often impressed by the use of sophisticated statistical techniques and complicated research designs so that those feminist sociologists who prefer qualitative, interactive, and experiential methods are often at a disadvantage in competing for funds. Commenting on the use of path models and regression analysis to explain the results of family violence scales, sociologist Mildred Pagelow noted the following in her testimony before Congressional subcommittees:

> It may seem glamorous to have paid interviewers go into the living rooms of thousands of American couples to count the number of times respondents remember and are willing to admit they slapped, hit, or kicked their spouses in the previous year. But what have we really learned about the interactional dynamics before and after those acts, the actual force of the acts, the damaged

sustained (or lack of it), and the cognitions
attached to the acts by both actor and receiver?
In actuality, very little (1979:345).

Underlying these problems is a fundamental conflict between the feminist agenda and the patriarchal values of government and private agencies (Nebraska Sociological Feminist Collective, 1983). In order to present the illusion of concern about women's issues, gatekeepers may award funding to those who conduct research "on" women (which views women solely and unreflectively as objects of the research process), and deny funding to those conducting research "for" women (which recognizes women's needs and aims at improving their actual circumstances) (Duelli-Klein, 1983). Thus, gatekeepers play into the hands of many "grant junkies" (Pagelow, 1979: 344) who are willing to capitalize on female oppression to advance their own careers while simultaneously "ripping-off the women's movement" (Stanley and Wise, 1983: 23).

Disseminating the Results

Publication is one of the most valued resources controlled by academic gatekeepers for several reasons. First, publication brings legitimation to the researcer and her ideas. Second, publication establishes the important topics and issues in the discipline and how they should be defined and investigated. Third, publication sets the style for those seeking publication and, as such, it influences generations of scholars.

Unfortunately, the publishing arena is also a context in which powerful gatekeepers can perpetuate their own ideas, approaches, and biases by excluding challenges from other scholars. Given women's marginal status in the discipline and the nature of feminism as "fundamentally subversive and critical" (Nebraska Sociological Feminist Collective, 1983), feminist sociologists are at a disadvantage in a system which rewards conformity to particular metaphysical and historical traditions.

For academic sociologists, publication in books and journals is the route to professional success. In the case of commercial publication, decisions about manuscripts are often based on a product's marketability rather than its substantive value (Spender, 1981b). For journal publications which rely on the method of "democratic peer review," the gatekeeping processes are different. Under the peer review system, unpaid evaluators, who remain anonymous to the author, read and judge a submitted article and recommend for or against its inclusion. Dale Spender has pointed out two ways in which this system allows the decision-making process to be influenced by non-substantive considerations (1981b). First, the selection of reviewers is not open but depends largely upon the editor's "contacts" and "friends," who usually "agree" on fundamental issues (1981: 195). Second, while names of reviewers remain anonymous, the names and institutional affiliations of the authors often do not, so that well-known scholars from prestigious institutions have an advantage over other colleagues. A third consideration is that the actual operation of the democratic peer review almost ensures that feminist work will not be published (Nebraska Sociological Feminist Collective, 1983). Given the exclusion of feminists from the mainstream of sociology and widespread ignorance about the present feminist discourse in the discipline, one's reviewer "peer" is likely to be poorly qualified to judge feminist scholarship. This was something discovered by Margrit Eichler (1981) when she submitted an article to the *Journal of Marriage and the Family* and received a review which criticized her use of "he/she" with the comment that "the language in the article is quite sexist."

Sometimes it is not reviewer's ignorance that negates their qualifications as evaluators, but their complete refusal to recognize research on women as valid scholarship. For example, a reviewer for *Sociological Quarterly* rejected a paper exploring the work of early women sociologists by beginning the evaluation with an observation "I suppose I'm biased, but I don't think this is sociology" (Nebraska Sociological Feminist Collective, 1983). Thus, a feminist sociologist might find that her work is judged by a fairly close network of reviewers who agree on certain theoretical and methodological issues, have achieved some degree of professional prestige and status themselves, and presumably have ideas and theories to "protect." These reviewers will likely know very little about feminist theory and research, even though some may have done research "on" women, and they will probably view basic feminist ontological assumptions with suspicion, if not outright disdain.

An additional issue must be addressed, and this is whether or not feminist journals and publishing houses are fundamentally different in the ways they evaluate the work of sociologists. According to Spender (1981b), with the exception of a few feminist journals which operate collectively and rotate decision-making positions, the answer is no. In her opinion, many feminist reviewers reject those articles which do not share their personal political beliefs and academic viewpoints. As a result, some scholars whose work is "too feminist" for mainstream journals find that they are criticized by reviewers from feminist journals for _not_ _being_ _feminist_ _enough_. For example, a reviewer for _Feminist_ _Studies_ clearly questioned the notion that important feminist scholarship regarding methodological issues was occurring in _any_ of the social sciences:

> ...(the author) deals with those feminist scholars who have situated themselves in relatively close proximity to their "disciplines"... and one could argue that the most important contributions have been entirely outside the mainstream social sciences.

Not only reviewers, but feminist editors can also manipulate the system to favor those articles of which they approve. Writing about her experiences as an editor Spender describes a familiar dilemma:

> If I like an article it is not difficult for me to "choose" two reviewers whom I suspect will also like it, and who will "justify" my assessment; by the same token, if I do not like it, it is not difficult to "choose" two reviewers who will not like it either. This hardly seems "objective" or even fair (1981b: 196).

Spender points out the need for feminist scholars to discuss gatekeeping issues among ourselves and in print.

We feel that some of the uncertainty about these issues revolves around two contradictory goals pursued by feminist sociologists and other feminist academicians. In addition to a third problem of successfully passing critical gatekeepers, feminist scholars are in the conflicting position of trying to become gatekeepers with a non-oppressive style while seeking alternatives to the present gatekeeping system. This is a difficult task given that we are asking feminists to invest in a system which they are simultaneously seeking to replace. Should we concentrate our efforts on achieving the gatekeeper status or direct our attention toward creating a new, more equitable system of evaluation? Can we expect a feminist scholar who has worked long and hard for her position as editor or reviewer to enthusiastically aid in dismantling the very hierarchy in which she now holds power? Are the two goals compatible within the career of one individual? These are difficult questions and they will require considerable public discussion before they are resolved.

Along these lines, some feminist sociologists have proposed strategies to ameliorate the difficulties we encounter with gatekeeping in the publishing process. For example, Jessie Bernard (1979) suggests such an approach called "intellectual confrontation," whereby space would be reserved in mainstream journals to point out carefully documented distortions and omissions and instances of sexism in articles and books reviewed by the journal over a period of time. The Nebraska Sociological Feminist Collective (1983) presents a variety of practical proposals including:

-- Recruiting non-academic research reviewers, especially members of the groups being studied;
-- Generating inter-disciplinary feminist reviews;
-- Formulating a policy of shared decision-making which provides editors and review boards with more input from readers and the general public;
-- Altering standards of scholarship to include controversy, emphasizing liberation, and stimulate action research;
-- Rotating key gatekeeping positions, including those of feminist scholars.

Finally, Dale Spender (1981) has proposed that feminist researchers begin to document the sex composition of the editors and advisory boards of journals in their discipline, as well as examine and report publicly on the nature of how those articles are accepted and rejected. As she explains, "When such material appears in print, it is quotable, it becomes reportable if not reputable by male standards. It enjoys the benefits of legitimation that accompany the printed word; we know this and should use it" (1981: 201).

Hiring, Promotion and Tenure

Closely related to the context of publishing is that of securing and maintaining an academic position. Given the current job market in sociology, recent Ph.D.s find it necessary to have one or more publications in order to be hired at an assistant professor level in a tenure-track position; once hired, promotion and tenure depend largely upon a scholar's publishing record. Thus, some of the features of gatekeeping in the publishing arena influence gatekeeping in the employment context.

One example of this can be found in an incident reported in a recent <u>SWS</u> (Sociologists for Women in Society) <u>Newsletter</u> (Nancy Shaw, etc., 1983). In this case, Nancy Stoller Shaw, a medical sociologist at the University of California, Santa Cruz, was denied tenure in the Community Studies faculty by the chancellor of her university. Significantly, every other campus committee that reviewed her record of teaching and research <u>recommended</u> <u>unanimously</u> that she be given tenure. It was the very nature of her work in areas such as the medicalization of childbirth and health care in women's prisons, which the chancellor found problematic. Once again, the argument that research on women is narrow and peripheral appears, as it did in the context of topic selection and publishing. The chancellor's internal memo spells it out clearly:

> The question is one of whether it is appropriate and desirable that such work be done by university faculty when it can just as well be done by journalists or persons employed by public service agencies. The university is the one institution chartered to undertake longer range research of basic scholarly significance...Such work may of course be directed toward specific problems. But, the primary aim of the work should be scholarship and the advancement of basic knowledge, not only the amelioration of the problem. This objective is seen to be grieviously lacking in Dr. Shaw's work (1983: 3, 20).

Of course, had Nancy Shaw's research been on men's prisons and adult male health care, the chancellor would very likely have reviewed these as acceptable mainstream criminology and medical sociology topics, and judged her work as contributing to the advancement of "basic knowledge."

Another feature of employment gatekeeping directed at feminists is not as prevalent in publishing, and it concerns the preference for social homogeneity among academic faculty. This often results in the establishment of two separate sets of criteria: one for the favored groups, and another for the undesirables. Such a pattern is illustrated in an example discussed by Laurel Richardson (1981) in which two sociologists were competing for the same tenure-track position. The first held her Ph.D. from a highly prestigious institution and was currently teaching at another prestigious university; her vita included numerous publications, fellowships, honors, and teaching awards. The second was a student at a mediocre university who had not yet started his dissertation research and had no fellowships, honors, teaching awards or independent teaching experience; his publications were all co-authored with his advisor and appeared in readers edited by his advisor. The personnel committee rejected the application of the woman with the following comments: "She hasn't published all *that* much;" "Why would she want to leave University X?" "I don't think she's married;" "I think she's older." Instead, the pre-dissertation student was invited for an interview because: "He's X's student and X always turns out good ones;" "He's promising;" "He'll make a good colleague;" "I think we could all live with him" (1981: 78). In this case, a female scholar who had ostensibly filled all the requirements necessary to pass employment gatekeepers (prestigious degree, numerous publications, excellence in teaching) was not judged according to those criteria. Instead, her marital status, age and motivation for the job were assessed, while the male candidate was evaluated for different qualities, such as his ability to "fit in" with the majority of the faculty and his link to his advisor.

This preference for homogeneity is also evident in attitudes regarding the hiring of lesbian and gay sociologists (ASA Task Group, 1982); 63% felt that hiring a known homosexual was not possible or would produce serious problems, while 83% felt the same was true if the person was a gay rights activist. Department chairs also perceived difficulty in promoting gay sociologists; 48% saw barriers to the promotion of known homosexuals, while 65% predicted problems with promoting activists. Interestingly, however, department heads perceived fewer problems with admitting or awarding degrees to homosexual students; 7% felt that awarding degrees to lesbian or gay students was not possible or would create serious difficulties, while the corresponding figure for faculty hiring, presented above, was 45%. This leads to a paradoxical conclusion: "Ironically, many heads and chairs thus feel free to train people they did not feel quite free to hire, once trained."

Other problems which gatekeeping in the employment context presents to feminist sociologists include: deciding whether or not to be "open" about one's feminist stance and dealing with sexism and sexist comments during the interviewing process (Ollenburger, 1983); managing the stigma of searching for an academic position while being a "local" whose spouse is already employed in the area (Zimmerman, 1983); and dealing with non- or anti-feminist women colleagues who are hired by male gatekeepers because of sexual and other unprofessional reasons (M. Thompson, 1983). As with the other contexts, we need more specific information on how these processes operate and how they are dealt with by feminist scholars.

Summary and Conclusions

The issues raised in this analysis are crucial to feminist sociologists because it is we who must safeguard the existing feminist discourse and stimulate its continued production. We cannot depend upon others, even our politically radical colleagues, to define and seriously analyze the oppression of women. As Cynthia Epstein observes, past history in our discipline confirms this fact so that "only since women sociologists have gained legitimation, visibility, and resources and have turned their attention to women themselves, has a new scholarship emerged" (1981: 154).

We would like to hear from feminist scholars in other disciplines about the nature of gatekeeping in their professions. Because of our commitment to viewing gatekeeping contextually, we suspect that some features of the process may be discipline-specific while others may be more universal. For example, topic selection may be an especially important context in sociology because the substantive parameters of sociology are more broadly defined than those of other fields such as economics or linguistics.

We suggested at the beginning of our analysis that focusing on actual practices and activities would uncover interrelations between gatekeeping in different contexts. Interestingly, these appeared as a pattern of circular (or mutually reinforcing) processes tying together actual practices within and between gatekeeping contexts. An example of a circular process <u>within</u> contexts is the situation in which the work of feminist scholars is not published so that they do not become reviewers, and because they do not become reviewers, the work of other feminist scholars does not get published. An example of a circular process <u>between</u> contexts is the mutually reinforcing defining of "mainstream" topics from which feminist concerns are excluded. Failure to legitimate the study of women as a topic means that researchers avoid it and no body of literature develops. At the funding level this absence of validating literature provides justification for evaluators who view feminist research proposals as "peripheral" and "specialized." In this circle, then, a feminist topic is rejected by funding gatekeepers because it lacks a tradition in the literature; but, one of the reasons for this missing tradition is the past refusal of gatekeepers to support such studies.

Our analysis, then, has revealed some gatekeeping practices (such as homogeneity and mutually reinforcing practices) which appear consistently in the activities of evaluation of scholars and scholarly production. However, we feel it important to recognize that there are no hard-and-fast rules in gatekeeping, at least for feminist sociologists. That is, even when we follow all the paths prescribed by those who control access to valued resources, we may <u>still</u> discover when it is our turn to be evaluated that the criteria for judgement have shifted. That is, gatekeepers do play by a set of rules, but one of these rules is that _all_ _rules_ _are_ _suspendable_, if this serves the purposes of the gatekeeper. Such a situation highlights the nature of gatekeeping as an often _arbitrary_ and _unpredictable_ process.

Given this, how can we as feminist scholars avoid being damaged by the gatekeeping system and learn to use it to our advantage? If the one rule is that there are no rules, can we learn to use a system based on power while we are still powerless? One logical answer is to put more feminists into gatekeeping positions and, thus, let the present system work for us. Then, at least, gatekeepers would be arbitrary _in_ _our_ _favor_ and social homogeneity would select us out for _acceptance_ rather than rejection. But we also need to address the issues that arise when _feminist_ gatekeepers evaluate the work of other scholars, both feminist and non-feminist. Finally, we must explore alternatives to the present gatekeeping system and search for more equitable ways of evaluating the scholarship of others. In particular, we need to be aware of the part that social relations play in determining the nature of scholarship in the social sciences, so that we may transform oppressive arrangements while redefining the nature of our discipline.

Bibliography

Acker, J. 1973. "Women and social stratification." American Journal of Sociology 78 (January): 936-45.
Adams, K.C. & N.C. Ware. 1979. "Sexism and the English language." Women: A Feminist Perspective, ed by J. Freeman. Palo Alto: Mayfield Press.
Addelson, K.P. 1983. "The man of professional wisdom." In Discovering Reality: Feminist Perspectives on Epistemology, Metaphysics, Methodology and Philosophy of Science, ed. by S. Harding and M. Hintikka. Boston: D. Reidel Publishing Co. Pp. 165-186.
Alderfer, H. (ed). 1980. Diary of a Conference on Sexuality. New York: Faculty Press.
Anderson, M. 1983. Thinking About Women. New York: Macmillan.
Astin, H. 1976. Some Action of Her Own. Lexington, MA: D.C. Heath.
Bart, P. 1971. "Sexism and social science." Journal of Marriage and the Family 33(November): 734-45.
Beck, E. 1982. Nice Jewish Girls: A Lesbian Reader. Watertown: Persephone Press.
Becker, H. 1963. Outsiders. New York: Free Press.
Bell, C. 1978. "Studying the locally powerful." Inside the Whale, ed. by C. Bell and S. Encel. London: Pergamon. Pp. 14 - 40.
Berger, P. 1967. The Sacred Canopy. Garden City, NY: Doubleday.
_____ and T. Luckmann. 1967. The Social Construction of Reality. New York: Doubleday and Company.
Bernard, J. 1981. The Female World. New York: Free Press.
_____. 1979. "Afterword." The Prism of Sex: Essays in the Sociology of Knowledge, ed. by Sherman and E. Beck. Madison: The University of Wisconsin, Press. Pp. 267-275.
_____. 1973. "My four revolutions." American Journal of Sociology 78(January): 773-91.
Berry, W. 1977. The Unsettling of America. New York: Free Press.
Blishen, B. R. 1976. "A revised socio-economic index for occupations in Canada." Canadian Review of Sociology and Anthropology 13: 71-79.
_____. 1969. Doctors and Doctrines. Toronto: University of Toronto Press.
Blum, A. 1977. "Criticalness and traditional prejudice." Canadian Journal of Sociology 2: 97-124.
Blumer, H. 1969. Symbolic Interactionism. Englewood Cliffs, NJ: Prentice-Hall.

Bohm, D. 1977. "Science as perception--communication." The Structure of Scientific Theories, edited by Frederick Suppe. Urbana: University of Illinois Press.
Boughey, H. 1978. The Insights of Sociology. Boston: Allyn and Bacon.
Brody, H. & D.S. Sobel. 1979. "A systems view of health and disease." Ways of Health, edited by David Sobel. New York: Harcourt, Brace and Jovanovich.
Bryan, J. 1973. "Occupational ideologies and individual attitudes of call girls." Deviance: The Interactionst Perspective, ed. by E. Rubington and M. Weinberg. London: Macmillan. Pp. 252-261.
Burgess, A. W., & Holmstrom, L. L. 1979a. "Rape: Sexual disruption and recovery". American Journal of Orthopsychiatry 49: 648-657.
_____. 1979b. "Adaptive strategies and recovery from rape". American Journal of Psychiatry 136: 1278-1282.
_____. 1974. "Rape trauma syndrome." American Journal of Psychiatry 131: 981-986.
Burtt, E. 1946. Right Thinking. New York: Random House.
Busch, L. 1980. "Structure and negotiation in agricultural sciences." Rural Sociology 45: 26-48.
Business Week. 1981. The Reindustrialization of America. June 1, p. 55.
Califia, Pat. 1980. Sapphistry. Tallahassee, FL: Naiad.
_____. 1981. "Feminism and sadomasochism." Heresies 3: 30-34.
Campbell, D.T. and D.W. Fiske. 1959. "Convergent and discriminant validation by the multitrait-multimethod matrix." Psychological Bulletin 56: 81-105.
Caplow, T. and R.J. McGee. 1958. The Academic Marketplace. Garden City, NY: Doubleday.
Carmen, E. H., Russo, N. F. and Miller, J. B. 1981. "Inequality and women's mental health: An overview." American Journal of Psychiatry 138: 1319-1330.
Chafe, W. 1972. The American Woman. New York: Oxford University Press.
Chesler, P. 1972. Women and Madness. Garden City, NY: Doubleday.
Chung, T. 1970. " A Chinese philosopher's theory of knowledge." Social Psychology Through Symbolic Interaction, ed. by G. Stone and H. Farberman. Waltham, MA: Xerox College Publishers. Pp. 121-139.
Cicourel, A. 1963. Cognitive Sociology. London: Longman.
Cixous, H. 1983. "The laugh of the medusa." The SIGNS Reader: Women, Gender and Scholarship, ed. by E. Abel and E.K. Abel. Chicago: University of Chicago Press. Pp. 279-297.

Clark, A. 1919. The Working Life of Women in the Seventeenth Century. London: G. Routledge and Sons.
Clarke, J. 1983. "Sexism, feminism and medicalism." Sociology of Health and Illness 5(Winter).
Conrad, P. and J. Schneider. 1980. Deviance and Medicalization. St. Louis: Mosby.
Cook, Judith A. 1984. "An interdisciplinary look at feminist methodology: Ideas and practice in sociology, history and anthropology." Humboldt Journal of Social Relations 10: 50-65.
_____ & M.M. Fonow. 1983. "Knowledge and women's interests." Presented at the 78th Annual Meeting of the American Sociological Association.
Cook, T.D. and D.T. Campbell. 1979. Quasi-experimentation. Boston: Houghton Mifflin.
Cooper, B.S. and D.P. Rice. 1976. "The economic cost of illness revisited." Social Security Bulletin (February): 31-36.
Cooperstock, R. and H. L. Lennard. 1979. "Some social meanings of tranquilizer use." Sociology of Health and Illness 1, #3: 331-347.
Corea, G. 1977. The Hidden Malpractice. New York: Jove/HBJ Books.
Coyner, S. 1980. "Women's studies as an academic discipline: Why and how to do it." Theories in Women's Studies ed. by G. Bowles and R. Duelli-Klein. Berkeley, CA: University of California. Pp. 18-40.
Daly, M. 1978. Gyn/Ecology. Boston: Beacon Press.
_____. 1973. Beyond God the Father. Boston: Beacon Press.
Daniels, A.K. 1975. "Feminist perspectives in sociological research." Another Voice, ed. by M. Millman and R.M. Kanter. Garden City, NY: Anchor Books. Pp. 340-80.
Davis, K. 1971. "Prostitution," Contemporary Social Problems, edited by R.K. Merton and R. Nisbet. New York: Harcourt Brace-Jovanovich. Pp. 341-351.
de Beauvoir, S. 1953. The Second Sex. Tr. H.M. Parshey. New York: Alfred Knopf.
Deegan, M.J. & M. Hill. 1987. Women and Symbolic Interaction. Waltham, MA: Allen and Unwin.
Deegan, M.J. 1985. "Multiple Minority Groups." In Women and Disability, ed. by M.J. Deegan and N.A. Brooks. New Brunswick, NJ: Transaction Books. Pp. 37-55.
Denzin, N. 1978. Sociological Methods. Toronto: McGraw-Hill.
Dill, B. 1983. "Race, class and gender: Prospects for an all inclusive sisterhood." Feminist Studies 9 (Spring): 131-150.

Dinnerstein, D. 1977. The Mermaid and the Minotaur. New York: Harper & Row.
Donnison, J. 1977. Midwives and Medical Men. London.
Donzelot, J. 1979. The Policing of Families. New York: Pantheon Books.
Doyal, L. 1979. The Political Economy of Health. London: Plutopress.
DuBois, B. 1983. "Passionate scholarship." In Theories of Women's Studies, ed. by G. Bowles and R. Klein. Boston: Routledge and Kegan Paul. Pp. 105-116.
Duelli-Klein, R. 1980. "How to do what we want to do: Thoughts about feminist methodology." In Theories in Women's Studies, ed. by G. Bowles and R. Duelli-Klein. Berkeley, CA: University of California. Pp. 48-64. (1983. Boston: Routledge and Kegan Paul.)
Dunnell, K. and A. Cartwright. 1972. Medicine Takers, Prescribers and Hoarders. London: Routledge, Kegan & Paul.
Durkheim, E. 1964. The Rules of Sociological Method. New York: The Free Press.
_____. 1951. Suicide. New York: The Free Press.
Dynes, R. 1974. "Sociology as a religious movement." American Sociologist 9(November): 169-76.
Ehrenreich, B. and D. English. 1978. For Her Own Good. New York: Anchor Books.
_____. 1973a. Witches, Midwives and Nurses. Old Westbury, NY: Feminist Press.
_____. 1973b. The Politics of Sickness. Old Westbury, NY: Feminist Press.
Ehrlich, C. 1971. "The male sociologist's burden." Journal of Marriage and the Family 33 (August): 421-30.
Eichler, M. 1981. "Power, dependency, love and the sexual division of labour." Women's Studies International Quarterly 4: 201-219
_____. 1980. The Double Standard: A Feminist Critique of Feminist Social Science. New York: St. Martin's Press.
Eisenstein, Z.R. 1979. "Developing a Theory of Capitalist Patriarchy." In Capitalist Patriarchy and the Case for Socialist Feminism, ed. by Z.R. Eisenstein. New York: Monthly Review Press. Pp. 5-40.
Ellis, E. M., Atkeson, B. M., & Calhoun, K. S. 1981. "An assessment of long-term reaction to rape". Journal of Abnormal Psychology 90: 263-266.
Elshtain, J.B. 1982. "Feminist discourse and its discontents: Language, power and meaning," Signs: Journal of Women in Culture and Society 7: 603-621.

Emslie, G. J. and Rosenfeld, A. 1983. "Incest reported by children and adolescents hospitalized for severe psychiatric problems." American Journal of Psychiatry 140: 708-711.
Engels, F. 1942. The Origins of the Family, Private Property and the State. New York: International Publishers.
Epstein, C.F. 1981. "Women in Sociological Analysis." In A Feminist Perspective in the Academy: The Difference It Makes, ed. by E. Langland and W.Gove. Chicago: The University of Chicago Press. Pp. 149-162
Faderman, L. 1981. Surpassing the Love of Men. New York: William Morrow.
Fee, E. 1975. "Women and health care." In Health and Medical Care in the U. S. V. Navarro (ed.). Farmingdale, NY: Baywood Pub. Co.
Feldman-Summers, S., Gordon, P. E., & Meagher, J. N. 1979. "The impact of rape on sexual satisfaction." Journal of Abnormal Psychology 88: 101-105.
Ferguson, Ann. 1981. "Patriarchy, sexual identity and the sexual revolution." Signs 7: 159-172.
Feyerabend, P.K. 1978. Science in a Free Society. London: Verso.
Fine, M. 1983. "'Taking control' across class lines: Coping with rape." Imagination, Cognition and Personality: The Scientific Study of Consciousness.
Firestone, S. 1970. The Dialectic of Sex. New York: Bantam.
Flexner, E. 1975. A Century of Struggle: The Women's Rights Movement in the United States. Cambridge: Harvard University Press.
Freeman, J. 1979. "The feminist scholar." Quest 5 (Summer): 26-36.
Freud, S. 1974. "Some psychical consequences of the anatomical distinctions between the sexes." Women and Analysis, ed. by J. Strouse. New York: Grossman. Pp. 17-26.
Friday, N. 1977. My Mother, My Self. New York: Delacorte.
Friedan, B. 1963. The Feminine Mystique. New York: Dell.
Frye, M. 1983. The Politics of Reality. The Crossing Press.
Gardner, M. 1983. "Great moments in pseudoscience." Asimov's Science Fiction Magazine 7(7): 67-77.
Garfinkle, H. 1967. Studies in Ethnomethodology. Englewood Cliffs, NJ: Prentice-Hall.
Gelles, R. J. 1972. The Violent Woman. Beverly Hills: Sage.
Gilligan, C. 1982. In a Different Voice. Cambridge,

Mass: Harvard University Press.
Glover, E. 1969. The Psychopathology of Prostitution. London: Institution for the Study and Treatment of Delinquency Publication.
Goffman, E. 1977. "The arrangement between the sexes." Theory and Society 4(Fall): 301-31.
_____. 1971. Relations in Public. New York: Basic Books
_____. 1963. Stigma. Englewood Cliffs, NJ: Prentice-Hall.
_____. 1961. Encounters: Two Studies in the Sociology of Interaction. Ind.: Bobbs-Merrill Co.
_____. 1961. Asylums. New York: Doubleday Anchor Books.
Gold, M. 1977. "A crisis of identity." Journal of Health and Social Behavior 18(June): 160-68.
Goldsmith, A. 1980. "Notes on the tyranny of language usage." Women's Studies International Quarterly 3 (2/3): 179-191.
Gornick, V. and B. Moran. 1971. Woman in Sexist Society. New York: Basic Books.
Gray, E.D. 1977. Green Paradise Lost. Welleseley, MA: Roundtable Press.
Greenwald, H. 1970. The Elegant Prostitute. New York: Walker and Company.
Gronau, R. 1973. "The measurement of output of the nonmarket sector." The Measurement of Economic and Social Performance. New York: National Bureau of Economic Research. Pp. 163-190.
Guajardo, H. 1980. The Phenomenology of Time Consciousness in the Life Cycle of a Mexican-American Woman. Master's Paper, Texas Woman's University.
Habermas, J. 1979. Communication and the Evolution of Society. Boston: Beacon Press.
_____. 1976. "A positively bisected rationalism." In The Positivistic Dispute in German Sociology, edited by T.W. Adorno, et al. New York: Harper & Row.
_____. 1973. Knowledge and Human Interests. Boston: Beacon Press.
Hacker, H. 1951. "Women as a minority group." Social Forces 30(September): 60-69.
Hanson, N. R. 1965. Patterns of Discovery. Cambridge: Cambridge at the University Press.
Harding, S. 1982. "Is gender a variable in conceptions of rationality? " Dialectica 36 (2-3): 226-242.
_____ and M. Hintikka, eds., 1983. Discovering Reality: Feminist Perspectives on Epistemology, Metaphysics, Methodology and Philosophy of Science. Dordrecht, Holland: D. Reidel Pub. Co.
Hare, N. and J. 1977. "Black male-female relationships." Transaction 7 (November-December): 65-68.

Hare-Mustin, R. 1983. "An appraisal of the relationship between women and psychotherapy." American Psychologist 38: 593-601.
Hartsock, N. 1983. "The Feminist Standpoint." Discovering Reality, ed. by S. Harding and M. Hintikka. Boston: D. Reidel Publishing Co. Pp. 56-77.
_____. 1979. "Feminist theory and the development of revolutionary strategy." In Capitalist Patriarchy and the Case for Socialist Feminism, ed. by Z.R. Eisenstein. New York: Monthly Review Press. Pp. 56-77.
Hays, H.R. 1964. The Dangerous Sex. New York: Pocket Books.
Heidegger, M. 1962. Being and Time. Trs. by J. MacQuarrie and E. Robinson. New York: Harper & Row.
Henriques, F. 1968. Modern Sexuality, Vol. III, Prostitution and Society. London: MacGibbon and Kee.
Henley, N. 1977. Body Politics. Englewood-Cliffs: Prentice Hall.
Herschberger, R. 1954. Adam's Rib. New York: Harper & Row.
Hersh, S.M. 1983. The Price of Power: Kissinger in the Nixon White House. New York: Summit Books.
Himelfarb, A. and C. J. Richardson. 1982. People, Power and Process Sociology for Canadians. Toronto: McGraw-Hill.
Hooks, B. 1981. Ain't I A Woman: Black Women and Feminism. Boston: South End Press.
Hough, K. and A. Bem. 1975. "Is the woman's movement erasing the mark of oppression from the female psyche?" Journal of Psychology 89: 249-58.
Hubbard, R. 1979. "Have only men evolved?" Women Looking at Biology Looking at Women, ed. by R. Hubbard, M. S. Henifen and B. Fried. Cambridge, MA: Schenkman.
_____ M. S. Henifen and B. Fried. Women Looking at Biology Looking at Women. Cambridge, MA: Schenkman.
Hughes, H.M. 1975. "Women in academic sociology." Sociological Focus 8 (August): 215-22.
Jaget, C., Ed. 1980. Prostitutes: Our Life. Bristol: Falling Wall Press.
Jespersen, O. 1965. The Philosophy of Grammar. New York: WW Norton & Co.
Juhasz, S. 1976. Naked and Fiery Forms: Modern American Poetry by Women: A New Tradition. New York:
Kanfer, S. 1972. "Sispeak: A misguided attempt to change herstory," Time, October 23: 79.
Kanter, R.M. 1977. Men and Women of the Corporation. New York: Basic Books.
Keller, E.F. 1982. "Feminism and science." Signs 7 (Spring): 589-601.

Kelly-Gadol, J. 1976. "The social relations of the sexes: Methodological implications of women's history." Signs (4): 809-23.
Kelman, E. and B. Staley. 1974. "The returning student: Needs of an important minority group." Eric Ed 103-747: 1-21.
Kerlinger, F.N. 1964. Foundations of Behavioral Research. New York: Holt, Rinehart and Winston.
Kessler, S. and W. McKenna. 1978. Gender: An Ethnomethodological Approach. New York: Wiley.
Kilpatrick, D.G., Resnick, P.A. & Vernon, L.J. 1981. "Effects of rape experience." Journal of Social Issues 37: 105-121.
Kirby, R. and J. Corzine. 1981. "The contagion of stigma: fieldwork among deviants." Qualitative Sociology 4 (1):3-20.
Klein, R.D. 1983. "How to do what we want to do: Thoughts about feminist methodology." Theories of Women's Studies, ed. by G. Bowles and R.D. Klein. Boston: Routledge and Kegan Paul.
Koedt, A. 1973. "The myth of the vaginal orgasm." In Radical Feminism, ed. by A. Koedt, E. Levine, and A. Rapone. NY: Quadrangle.
Koss, M.P. 1983. "The scope of rape: Implications for the clinical treatment of victims." The Clinical Psychologist 36 (summer): 88-91.
Kuhn, T.S. 1970. The Structure of Scientific Revolutions. Chicago: University of Chicago Press.
Kutza E.A. 1981. "Benefits for the disabled: how beneficial for women?" Women and Disability, ed. by M.J. Deegan and N. Brooks. New Brunswick, NJ: Transaction Press. Pp. 68-86.
Ladner, J. 1973. The Death of White Sociology. New York: Random House.
Lakoff, R. 1975. Language and Women's Place. New York: Harper & Row.
Lauderdale, P. 1976. "Deviance and moral boundaries." Amercian Sociological Review 41: 660-676.
Leeds Revolutionary Feminist Group. 1975. Editors. Love Your Enemy? London: Onlywomen Press.
Leffler, A., D.L. Gillespie and E. Lerner. 1973. Academic Feminists and the Women's Movement. AcaFem, Iowa City.
Leidig, M.W. 1981. "Violence against women: A feminist-psychological analysis." In Female Psychology: The Emerging Self, 2nd Ed, ed. by S. Cox. New York: St. Martin's Press.
Lerner, G. 1979. The Majority Finds its Past: Placing Women in History. New York: Oxford University Press.

_____. 1972. Black Women in White America: A Documentary. New York: Pantheon.
Lewis, J. 1981. The Politics of Motherhood. London: Croom Helm.
Lippard, Lucy. 1973. From the Centre: Feminist Essays on Women's Art. New York: Dutton.
Lorber, J. 1975. "Women and medical sociology." Another Voice, ed. by M. Millman and R. Kanter. New York: Anchor.
Lowe, M. and R. Hubbard, eds. 1983. Woman's Nature: Rationalization of Inequality. The Athene Series. Elmsford, NY: Pergammon Press.
McCormack, T. 1975. "Toward a non-sexist perspective on social and political change." Another Voice, ed. by M. Millman & R.M. Kanter. New York: Anchor Books. Pp. 1-33.
McDaniel, J. 1978. "The transformation of silence into language and action," Sinister Wisdom 6: 4-25.
McDonald, L. 1975. "Wages of work." Canadian Forum (April/May): 4-7.
McHugh, P. et al. 1974. On the Beginning of Social Inquiry. London: Routledge and Kegan Paul.
MacKinnon, C.A. 1983. "Feminism, Marxism, method and the state: Toward feminist jurisprudence." Signs 8:(Summer): 635-658.
_____. 1982. "Feminism, Marxism, method and the state: An agenda for theory." Signs 7 (Spring): 515-44.
McRobbie, A. 1982. "The politics of feminist research: Between talk, test and action." Feminist Review, 12: 45-68.
Malhotra, V. A. 1977. "Mead's theory of self and phenomenology: An empirical analysis." The Wisconsin Sociologist 14: 1-
_____ and J.L. Deneen. 1982. "Power-saturated vs. appreciative conversations among children and adults. Paper presented at the 10th World Congress of Sociology. Mexico City.
Marx, Karl. 1967. Das Kapital, Vol. I. ed by F. Engels. Trans. by S. Moore and E. Avelzng. New York: International Pub.
Meacham, J.A. 1980. "Research on remembering: Interrogation or conversation, monologue, or dialogue?" Human Development 23: 236-45.
Mead, G. H. 1959. The Philosophy of the Present. LaSalle, IL: Open Court Press.
_____. 1938. The Philosophy of the Act. Chicago: University of Chicago Press.
Merton, R.K. 1973. The Sociology of Science. Chicago: University of Chicago Press.

Mies, M. 1978. "Methodische postulate zur frauenforschung - Dargestellt am beispiel der gewalt gegen Frauen (Methodological postulates for women's studies - exemplified through a project dealing with violence against women)." Beitrage zur Feministichen Theorie und Praxis 1: 41-64.
Miller, D.L. 1973. George Herber Mead: Self, Language and the Social World. Austin: University of Texas Press.
Millett, K. 1971. Sexual Politics. Garden City, NY: Doubleday.
Millman, M. and R.M. Kanter. 1975. Another Voice: Feminist Perspectives on Social Life and Social Science. New York: Anchor Books.
Mills, C.W. 1959. The Sociological Imagination. New York: Oxford University Press.
_____. 1943. "The professional ideology of social pathologists." American Journal of Sociology 49 (September): 165-180.
Morgan. R. 1980. "Theory and practice: Pornography and rape." Take Back the Night, edited by L. Lederer. New York: William Morrow.
Moynihan, D.P. 1970. "Memo to Nixon on the status of negroes, January 16, 1970." New York Times, 1 March.
_____. 1965. The Negro Family: the Case for National Action. U.S. Dept. of Labor, Washington D.C.
Muller, C. 1979. "Methodological issues in health economics research relevant to women." Social Science and Medicine 2: 819-25.
Mullins, N. C. 1973. Theory and Theoretical Groups in Contemporary American Sociology. New York: Harper & Row.
Murdrick, N.R. 1983. "Disabled women." Society 20 (March/April): 51-56.
Myron, N. & C. Bunch. 1975. Lesbianism and the Women's Movement. Baltimore: Diana Press.
Nadel, S.F. 1951. The Foundations of Social Anthropology. Glencoe, IL: Free Press.
"Nancy Shaw denied tenure at UC Santa Cruz." 1979. SWS Newsletter 13: 3,20.
Navarro, V. 1975. "Women in healthcare." New England Journal of Medicine 292(8): 398-402.
Nebraska Sociological Feminist Collective (C. Trainor, B.Hartung, J.C. Ollenburger, H.A. Moore and M.J. Deegan). 1983. "A feminist ethic for social science research."Women's Studies International Forum 6: 535-543.
Nestle, J. 1981. "Butch-fem relationships." Heresies 3: 21-24.

Nilsen, A.P. 1973. "The correlations betweem gender and other semantic features in American English." Paper delivered to the Linguistic Society of America.
Nobel, J.H., Jr. 1977. "The limits of cost-benefit analysis as a guide to priority setting in rehabilitation." Evaluation Quarterly 1(3): 347-380.
Nunnally, J.C. and R.L. Durham. 1975. "Validity, reliability, and special problems of measurement in evaluation research." Handbook of Evaluation Research, Vol. I, ed. by E.L. Struening and M. Guttentag. Beverly Hills: Sage.
Oakley, A. 1981. "Interviewing women: A contradiction in terms." Doing Feminist Research, ed. by H. Roberts. London & Boston: Routledge and Kegan Paul. Pp. 30-61.
_____. 1976. "Wise women and medicine man." The Rights and Wrongs of Women, ed. by J.Mitchell and A. Oakley. Harmondsworth, Mddx.: Penguin Books.
_____. 1974. The Sociology of Housework. New York: Pantheon Books.
Off Our Backs August/September 1983.
Ogilvy, J. 1979. Many Dimensional Man. New York: Harper & Row.
Ollenburger, J.C. 1983. "Feminists on the job market: A personal account." The Midwest Feminist Papers 3: 49-52.
Orlando, L. 1982. "Bad girls and 'good' politics." Village Voice Literary Supplement 13,1: 161-9.
Owens, L. 1981. "'Doing nothing': The effects of keeping time schedules on research participants." Paper presented at the Fall Sociological Research Symposium: East Texas State University.
Pagelow, M.D. 1979. "Research on woman battering." In Stopping Wife Abuse, ed. by J.B. Fleming. Garden City, NY: Anchor Press.
Palmer, P. 1983. "White women/Black women: The Dualism of female identity and experience in the United States." Feminist Studies 9 (Spring): 151-170.
Parlet, M. and G. Dearden, eds., 1977. Introduction to Illuminative Evaluation: Studies in Higher Education. Caradiff-by-Sea, CA: Pacific Sounding Press.
_____ and D. Hamilton, 1978. "Evaluation as illumination: A new approach to the study of innovatory programs." Beyond the Numbers Game, ed. by D. Hamilton, et al. London: McMillan. Pp. 6-22.
Parsons, T. 1951. The Social System. Glencoe, IL: Free Press.

_____ and R. Bales. 1955a. "Illness, therapy and the modern urban American family." Journal of Social Issues 8: 32-44.
_____. 1955b. Family, Socialization and Interaction Process. Glencoe, Ill: The Free Press.
Pederson, D., M. Shindeling & D. Johnson. 1975. "Effects of sex of examiner on children's quantitative test performance." Women: Dependent or Independent Variable?, ed. by R. Unger and F. Denmark. NY: Psychological Dimensions. Pp. 409-416.
Penelope, J. 1978. "Sexist grammar." College English 40 (3): 800-811.
Pfohl, S. 1977. "The discovery' of child abuse." Social Problems 24(February): 310-23.
Pfuhl, E. 1980. The Deviance Process. New York: D. Van Nostrand Co.
Pinchbeck, I. 1969. Women Workers and the Industrial Revolution, 1750-1850. London: Frank Cass.
Project Courtwatch. 1980. Franklin County Common Pleas Court: A Feminist View. Columbus, OH: Women Against Rape.
Radicalesbians. 1972. "The woman-identified woman." Out of the Closets, ed. by Jay and Young. New York: Douglas Book Corp.
Rainwater, L. and W.L. Yancey. 1967. The Moynihan Report and the Politics of Controversy. M.I.T. Press, Cambridge, MA.
Reinharz, S. 1984. On Becoming a Social Scientist. New Brunswick: Transaction Press.
_____. 1985. "Feminist distrust: Problems of context and content in sociological work." Exploring Clinical Methods for Social Research, ed. by Berg and Smith. Beverly Hills: Sage Publications. Pp.153-72.
Resick P.A., K.S. Calhoun, B.M. Atkeson, and E.M. Ellis. 1981. "Social adjustment in victims of sexual assault." Journal of Consulting and Clinical Psychology 49 : 705-12.
Rich, A. 1976. Of Woman Born. New York: Norton.
_____. 1980. "Compulsory heterosexuality and lesbian existence." Signs 5: 631-660.
Richardson, L.W. 1981. The Dynamics of Sex and Gender: A Sociological Perspective. Boston: Houghton Mifflin.
Ritzer, G. 1975. "Sociology." American Sociologist 10: 156-167.
Roberts, B. 1983. "Phallusies of sociobiology: A feminist critique." Unpublished manuscript.

Roberts, H. 1981a. "Some of the boys won't play anymore: the impact of feminism on sociology." Men's Studies Modified: The Impact of Feminism on Academic Disiplines, ed. by D. Spender. Elmsford, NY: Pergamon Press. Pp. 73-83.

_____, ed. 1981b. Doing Feminist Research. London: Routledge & Kegan Paul.

Rorty, R. 1980. "Pragmatism, relativism, and irrationalism." Proceedings and Addresses of the American Philosophical Association. 53 (6): 719-38.

Rossi, A.S. and A. Calderwood. 1973. Academic Women on the Move. Russell Sage Foundation, New York.

Rowbotham, S. 1973. Woman's Consciousness, Man's World. Baltimore: Penguin Books.

_____, L. Segal and H. Wainwright. 1979. Beyond the Fragments: Feminism and the Making of Socialism. London: Merlin Press.

Russell, D.E.H. and N. Howell. 1983. "The prevalence of rape in the United States revisited." Signs 8: 689-95.

Ryan, W. 1972. Blaming the Victim. New York: Vintage Books.

Schaef, A. W. 1979. Talk given at the University. of Missouri-Kansas City.

Scheff, T. 1966. Being Mentally Ill. Chicago: Aldine.

Schneider, J. W. and S. L. Hacker, 1973. "Sex role imagery and the use of the generic 'man' in introductory texts." American Sociologist, 8(February): 12-18.

Schur, E. 1980. The politics of deviance. Englewood Cliffs, NJ: Prentice-Hall.

Schutz, A. 1970. On Phenomenology and Social Relations. Ed. by H.R. Wagner. Chicago: University of Chicago Press.

Scott, R. 1969. The Making of Blind Men. New York: Russell Sage Foundation.

Scully, D. 1980. Men Who Control Women's Health. Boston: Houghton Mifflin Co.

Shapiro, J., C. Secor and A. Butchart, 1983. "Illuminative evaluation: Assessment of the transportability of a management training program for women in higher education." Educational Evaluation and Policy Analysis, 5(4): 456-471.

Sherman, L. W. 1974. "Uses of the masters." American Sociologist 9(November): 176-81.

Shields, S. A. 1982. "The variability hypothesis." Signs 7 (Summer): 769-97.

Sieber, S. D. 1973. "The integration of fieldwork and survey methods." American Journal of Sociology 78(May): 1335-39.
Silvira, J. 1980. "Generic masculine words and thinking." Women's Studies International Quarterly 3 (2/3):165-178.
Simmons, M. 1979. "Racism and feminism: A schism in the sisterhood." Feminist Studies 5(Summer):
Sissman, L.E. 1972. "Plastic English." Atlantic Monthly (October): 32, 34, 37.
Sjorberg, G. 1975. "Politics, ethics, and evaluation research." Handbook of Evaluation Research, Vol. II, ed. by M. Guttentag and E. L. Struening. Beverly Hills: Sage.
Skinner, B.F. 1971. Beyond Freedom and Dignity. New York: Alfred Knopf.
Slocum, S. 1980. "Woman the gatherer: male bias in anthropology." Issues in Feminism, edited by S. Ruth. Boston: Houghton Mifflin. Pp. 214-221.
Smart, C. 1976. Women, Crime and Criminology. London: Routledge and Kegan Paul.
Smith, D. 1983. "The renaissance of women." Keynote Address, Canadian Research Institute for the Advancement of Women.
_____. 1979. "A sociology for women." The Prism of Sex: Essays in the Sociology of Knowledge, ed. by J. Sherman and E.T. Beck. Madison, WI: University of Wisconsin Press.
_____. 1978. "A peculiar eclipsing: Women's exclusion from man's culture." Women's Studies International Quarterly 1: 281-296.
_____. 1977. Feminism and Marxism. Canada.
_____. 1976. "Some implications of a sociology for women." Women in a Man-Made World, 2nd Ed., ed. by N. Glazer and H.Y. Waehrer. Chicago: McNally. Pp. 15-29.
_____. 1975. "An analysis of ideological structures and how women are excluded." Canadian Review of Sociology and Anthropology 12 (No. 14, pt. 1): 353-69.
_____. 1974a. "Women's perspective as a radical critique of sociology." Sociological Inquiry, 44 (#1): 7-13.
_____. 1974b. "The ideological practice of sociology." Catalyst 8 (Winter): 39-56.
Spector, M. and J. Kitsuse. 1979. Constructing Social Problems. Menlo Park, CA: Benjamin/Cummings.
Speier, M. 1973. How to Analyze Everyday Conversation. Pacific Palisades: Goodyear Press.

Spender, D. 1981a. Men's Studies Modified: The Impact of Feminism on Academic Disciplines. Emsford, NY: Pergamon Press.
_____. 1981b. "The gatekeepers: A feminist critique of academic publishing." Doing Feminist Research, ed. by H. Roberts (ed.),. Boston: Routledge and Kegan Paul.
_____. 1980. Man Made Language. London: Routledge and Kegan Paul.
Stable, C. 1981. "An analysis of the effects of writing daily journals." Paper presented at the Fall Sociological Research Symposium: East Texas State University.
Stanley, L. and S. Wise. 1983. Breaking Out: Feminist Consciousness and Feminist Research. London & Boston: Routledge and Kegan Paul.
Steinem, G. 1980. "Erotica and pornography: A clear and present difference." Take Back the Night, edited by L. Lederer. New York: William Morrow.
Steinmetz, S. K. 1974. "The sexual context of social research." American Sociologist 9(August): 111-16.
Stimpson, C.R. 1980. "Power, presentations, and the presentable." Issues in Feminism, ed. by S. Ruth. Boston: Houghton Mifflin. Pp. 426-440.
Suppe, F. 1977. "The search for philosophic understanding of scientific theories." The Structure of Scientific Theories, ed. by F. Suppe. Urbana: University of Illinois Press.
Symonds, M. 1980. "The 'second jury' to victims." Evaluation and Change. Special Edition: 36-38.
Szasz, T. 1966. The Myth of Mental Illness. New York: Dell.
_____. 1976. "Mercenary psychiatry." The New Republic 174(13 March): 10-12.
"Task Group on Homosexuality Report Published." 1982. ASA Footnotes 10: 1, 12.
Terman, L. M. et al. 1925. Genetic Studies of Genius. Vol. 1. Standford, CA: Standford University Press.
Tetreault, P. and A.R. Esper. 1983. "Attitudes toward rape and jurors' verdicts." Paper presented at the Ninth Annual Conference of the Association for Women in Psychology. Seattle, WA: March.
Thompson, D. 1983. Over Our Dead Bodies. London: Virago.
Thompson, M. 1983. "Sexual oppression and women sociologists." The Midwest Feminist Papers 3: 70-75.
Thornton-Dill, B. 1983. "On the hem of life: Race, class and prospects for sisterhood." Class, Race and Sex, edited by A. Swerdlow & H. Lesslinger. Boston: G.K. Hall & Co. Pp. 173-188.

Tolpin, M. 1984. "Wheaton's assessment process: A case study and its lessons." In Toward a Balanced Curriculum, ed. by B. Spanier et al. Cambridge, MA: Schenkman Pub. Co. Pp. 173-88.
Tressemer, D. 1975a. "Assumptions made about gender roles." Another Voice, ed. by Millman and Kanter. NY: Anchor Books.
_____. 1975b. "Measuring sex differences." Sociological Inquiry 45 (4): 308-309.
_____. 1974. "Fear of success." Psychology Today 7 (10): 82-85.
Trow, M.A., 1970. "Methodological problems in the evaluation of innovation." In M.C. Wittrock and D.E. Wiley, (eds), The Evaluatiin of Instruction. New York: Holt, Rinehart and Winston. Pp. 289-305.
Tuchman, G., A.K. Daniels and J. Benet, eds. 1978. Hearth and Home. New York: Oxford University Press.
_____ & H. Tuchman. 1980. "Women as part time faculty members in higher education." Higher Education 10 (2): 169-179.
Tyler, F.B., K.I. Pargament, and M. Gatz. 1983. "The resource collaborator role: A model for interactions involving psychologists." American Psychologist 38: 388-98.
U.S. Bureau of the Census. 1984. Statistical Abstract of the United States. Washington, D.C.: U.S. Government Printing Office. Table 114.
Van den Berghe, P. 1970. Academic Gamesmanship: How to Make a Ph.D Pay. Abelard-Schuman, New York.
Vetter, B. M. 1976. "Women in the natural sciences." Signs 1(Spring): 713-9.
Walker, L.E. 1979. The Battered Woman. New York: Harper Colophon Books.
Walkowitz, J. 1980. Prostitution and Victorian Society. London & New York: Cambridge University Press.
Wallace, M. 1978. Black Macho and the Myth of the Superwoman. Dial Press, New York.
Walum, L. R. 1977. The Dynamics of Sex and Gender. Chicago: Rand McNally.
The Washington Post. 1984. "Economic stress surfacing late in 1984." (3 June).
Weber, M. 1947. The Methodology of the Social Sciences. Glencoe, IL: Free Press.
Welch, M. & S. Lewis. 1980. "Mid-decade assessment of sex biases in placement of sociology Ph.D.s: Evidence for contextual variation." American Sociologist 15 (August): 120-127.
Westkott, M. 1979. "Feminist criticism in the social sciences." Harvard Educational Review 49 (4): 422-430.

Williams, J.E. and K.A. Holmes. 1981. The Second
    Assault: Rape and Public Attitudes. Westport, CN:
    Greenwood Press.
Willis, E. 1981. "Nature's revenge." The New York Times
    Book Review July 12: 9,18,19.
Winch, P. 1977. "The idea of a social science."
    Understanding and Social Inquiry edited by Dallmayr
    and McCarthy. Notre Dame, Ind.: Notre Dame Press.
Winn, D. 1974. Prostitutes. London: Hutchinson.
Zimmerman, M. 1983. "The dual sociologist marriage."
    The Midwest Feminist Papers 3: 56-59.
Zita, J. 1981. "Historical amnesia and the lesbian
    continuum" Signs 7: 172-187.

Contributors' Notes

PAULINE B. BART is professor of sociology in the departments of psychiatry and sociology at the University of Illinois. She has recently co-authored *Stopping Rape: Successful Survival Strategies* which compares women who were attacked and avoided rape with those who were raped. *The Student Sociologist's Handbook* is now in its fourth edition, published by Random House. Currently, Dr. Bart is studying the effect of women taking self-defense on self concept and experiences, and, on the Macro level, the impact of the revised Illinois Sexual Assault statute. She was a visiting scholar at Harvard Law School and UCLA Law School where she studied feminist jurisprudence with Catharine A. MacKinnon. Her concern with conditions facilitating violence against women has led her to work as an anti-pornographer researcher and activist. She has two granddaughters, but is less optimistic than she used to be about the probability of their growing up in a world where women are not subordinated. She is still an activist in what is left of the Women's Liberation Movement.

ANN BRISTOW currently co-directs the Women's Health and Learning Center, the first and only multi-disciplinary health project providing services to women prisoners in the United States. Working in Massachusetts women's prison at Framingham, Dr. Bristow also directs a project investigating battering and sexual violence in the lives of incarcerated women. Other research and publications are in the area of women's experiences of victimization. As a clinical psychologist, she offers expert testimony in cases of rape and battered women who have killed in self-defense.

JUANNE N. CLARKE currently is studying sex differences in spousal adaptation to cancer. This is a sequel to her book, It's Cancer: The Personal Experiences of Women Who Have Received a Cancer Diagnosis. She currently is employed as Associate Professor of Sociology at Wilfrid Laurier University, Waterloo, Ontario, where she teaches medical sociology, sociology of health and illness, and methodological issues in social science.

JUDITH A. COOK is Director of the Thresholds Psychiatric Rehabilitation Research Institute, Chicago, Illinois, and a Field Faculty member of the School of Social Service Administration of the University of Chicago. She has published research in the areas of familial reactions to childhood cancer, gender differences in teaching styles of university professors, lawyer-social work conflict in juvenile court, and parental burden in coping with offspring's chronic mental illness. Her current research includes studies of vocation transition among mentally ill adolescents, and the effects of opening sealed adoption records. Dr. Cook has completed a book on Feminist Epistemology and Methodology with Mary Margaret Fonow.

MARY JO DEEGAN is an associate professor of sociology at the University of Nebraska--Lincoln. She has worked periodically with the Nebraska Feminist Sociology Collective for the last eight years. Her areas of specialization include theory, history of science, medical sociology, and qualitative methods. She is the coeditor with Nancy Brooks of Women and Disability; coeditor with Michael Hill of Women and Symbolic Interaction; and author of Jane Addams and the Men of the Chicago School, 1892-1918. Her next project is a feminist theory text.

JODY ESPER is assistant professor of psychology at Valparaiso University in Valparaiso, Indiana. She received her Ph.D in Social Cognition and the Psychology of Women from Kansas State University. Her current research interest involves investigating the effects that well-formed cognitive structures related to rape knowledge (attitudes, beliefs, etc.) have on the processing of information about the victims of rape. Dr. Esper is also still involved in work related to the documentation of the long-term effects of rape on women's psychological functioning and life-style and is in the early stages of writing a book based on her research in the area.

MARY MARGARET FONOW is a Sociologist and Research Associate with the Center for Women's Studies at the Ohio State University. Currently, she is conducting research on rape education and the effects of economic dislocation on women steelworkers. She is editing (with Judith A. Cook) a volume on feminist approaches to research. Her areas of specialization are women and work, poverty and public policy.

BETH HARTUNG is Assistant Professor of Sociology at California State University at Fresno. Her research interests include the human consequences of academic labor market stratification, the underemployment of professionals and other labor market questions. She is currently studying the divergence of contemporary social movements from The Left (with Peter Kivisto). She teaches women's studies, social psychology, popular culture and ever-popular general studies courses.

JUDITH A. LEVY is Assistant Professor of Health Resources Management at the School of Public Health, University of Illinois, Chicago. Her research interests include social movements in medicine, aging and the life course, and disability and rehabilitation. She currently is a post-doctoral fellow of the Midwest Council for Social Research on Aging.

VALERIE MALHOTRA is writing a monograph about the effect of childhood trauma on women's lives, based on the diaries and autobiographies discussed in her chapter in this collection. She has recently written an article on Heidegger and Mead (forthcoming in Human Studies) which attempts to reground social psychology in an existentialist ontology. Dr. Malhotra is Associate Professor in the Department of Sociology and Social Work at Texas Women's University, the largest women's university in the world. She is also licensed as a counselor, as a certified clinical sociologist by the Association for Sociological Practice, and as Certified Social Worker - Advanced Clinical Practitioner. Her areas of specialization include sociological theory, qualitative research methods, social psychology, sociology of music and sociological practice.

HELEN A. MOORE is associate professor of Sociology and Chair of the Women's Studies Program at the University of Nebraska-Lincoln. She is interested in feminist education inside and outside of the academy and is active with the National Women's Studies Association. Her research interests include women, minorities and the political economy of schooling and work. Currently she is studying the intersection of racism, classism and sexism in vocational training at two-year colleges.

JANE C. OLLENBURGER is assistant professor of Sociology at the University of Minnesota-Duluth. Her areas of teaching include the Sociology of Women, Criminology and Research Methods. In research, her most recent projects include research on family violence as well as an international project reviewing programs which reduce fear of crime among the elderly.

JULIA PENELOPE is an associate professor of English who is on an unpaid leave from the University of Nebraska--Lincoln. She is looking for investors for a new publishing company, Warexx Worxx, and she is the creator of the Dyke "Trivia" Game. Her areas of academic specialization include feminist theory, lesbian ethics, linquistics, and literature. She is the coeditor with Susan Wolfe of The Coming Out Stories and is working with Morgan Gray on a manuscript called The Book of Found Goddesses.

BETH REED, Director or the National Summer Institute in Women's Studies described in this collection, has established a unique Women's Studies program that provides resources for faculty in twelve colleges and sponsors a national institute. The institute began in 1975 with a strong committee of feminist colleagues. She is currently a Fellow of the Assembly of Scholars at the Schomberg Center for Research in Black Culture as well as a freelance journalist.

JOAN POLINER SHAPIRO is Co-Director of Women's Studies and Adjunct Assistant Professor of Education at the University of Pennsylvania. Much of her published work has been concerned with applying feminist methodology to educational processes, and with studying the role of women in education. Her most recent article, "Women in Education: At Risk or Prepared?" will be published in <u>The Educational Forum</u> (Winter, 1987). She continues to write on the evaluation of Women's Studies programs and projects. She is also working on ethical issues in Women's Studies.

CAROL SMART is currently lecturer in Sociology at the University of Warwick, U.K. Her main areas of teaching are women's studies, social problems and the sociology of law. Dr. Smart's recent research has been in the field of women and family law which resulted in the book, <u>The Ties That Bind: Law, Marriage and the Reproduction of Patriarchal Relations</u> (1984). More recently she has co-edited <u>Women in Law</u> (1985) with Julia Brody. She is currently working on a book on feminist perspectives on law.

DOROTHY E. SMITH is professor in the Department of Sociology in Education at the Ontario Institute for Studies in Education, Toronto, Canada, specializing in feminist epistemology in the social sciences and in the social organization of knowledge (from a feminist standpoint). My thinking since I became active in the women's movement has been focused on problems of how to grasp the macro-relations of power from the standpoint of women's experience. Theorizing developed out of practical experience of organizing with women, particularly around the development of feminist research strategies for women outside the academy and approaches to women's studies. My book on The Everyday World as Problematic: A Feminist Sociology (forthcoming, September 1987, Northeastern University Press) takes up methods of thinking about these relations and processes systematically. Currently I am researching with Allison Griffith the work mothers do in relation to their children's schooling, using an approach based on this.

MARY WHITE STEWART is currently Dean of the School of Humanities at Old College, Reno, Nevada, a private college with both a Humanities and a Law School. Although the majority of her time is spent on accreditation, program development, she remains interested in Women's Studies, family and deviance. She is currently working on two related pieces of research; a study of the portrayal of anger on prime time television and a study of the relationship between anger and life situations among the elderly.

VERA WHISMAN is a PH.D candidate in sociology at New York University, at work on a dissertation comparing the identity accounts of lesbians and gay men. She teaches courses in gender and in sexuality, and has worked to establish an undergraduate Women's Studies program at New York University.

Index

Black wimmin   6,11,54-66,181-182,193-194
    myth of matriarchy   59-60
    working class   56-57,65,181-182
Capitalism   23,25-31,33,56-57,60-62
Civil rights   38,60-62,188,193
Class   26-27,32,55-56,59-66,78-79,146,161,165-167,
    180-181,193-194
    and race   8,59,63-66,148
Consciousness raising   70-76,79-81,187-189
Construct validity   141-143,145,152-157
Contagious Diseases Act   37
Cross-sex research   8,44-46
Economics   23-31,144-145
    division of labor   29-31,144-145
    inequality   9-12,39-41,55-57,64-65
Education   13-15,21-22,104-105,107-108,165-167,187-188
Ethic
    code of   2-4,19-22,52-53
    definition   1,19-22,24-25,76
    feminist   1,4-5,13-14,18-19,60-66,71-72,84-87,
        104-106,164-165,170
    lesbian   48-53
    problems   39-46,140
Evaluation research   100,110-112
Feminist methodologies   48-49,72,100,111-112,140-141,
    159-161,170-173,210-212
    activist/advocacy   7-9,23-27,37-38,48-50,76-81,84-85,
        104-105,165-167,170,198-200
    collaborative   70-71,84-85,88-90,110-112,114-115
    communicative competency   83-84,87

Feminist methodologies (continued)
    illuminative   103-105,114-116
    interviews   19-20,42,45-46,70-74,76-78,100,111-112
    triangulation   82,88-89,171-173
Feminist theory   23-25,189-195
    criticisms of,   26-30,65-66,179-183
    critique of patriarchy   8,10,24-27,34-35,48,68-69,73,
        100-103,115,143-148,151-157,159,178,203-206
Freud   121,178,191
Funding   16-18,102,206-297,217
Gatekeeping   13-18,21-22,100-101,195-200,201-217
    feminist   19-22,115-116,209-212,216-217
Gender   26-27,120-121,125-126,129,146-148
    antitheses   24-27,30-31
    femininity   24,120,125-126,128-129
    masculinity   24.31-33,125-126,128-129,130-134
Generic "man"   9-13,119-125,131-132,148
Health   158,160,162-164,213
Heterosexism/homophobia   11-12,32,49,108,174-175,178-179
Language   9-13,21,24.148-152
    feminist   21,122
    patriarchal   9-13,121-138,148-152
    neutral   122-124,137-138
Lesbian   11-12,48-53,174-186,194,214
Marxism/Marx   23,26-28,193-194
Medical model   68-70,162-164
National Summer Institute in Women's Studies
        105-108,113-114
Objectification of wimmin   4-5,8,19-20,84-85,101-102
Objectivity   4-5,10,13,15-16,104-105,123-124,
        137-138,149-150

Patriarchal
    academy   4,16,109,188-189,197-199,201-217
    methodologies 9-14,19,68-73,100-103,139-140,
        142-148,152-156,178,200-204
    organization   1,24-26
Peace movement   26,188
Physically challenged wimmin   5,16-17,145,148
Pornography   174-186
Positivism   12-13,139-140,148-152,162-164,170-172
Prescribed passivity   131-133,150-152
Prostitution   37-46
Publication   16-18,21-22,58,134,208-212
Public policy   11,16-18,28,32,37-39,40,54-55,61-65,
        144-145,206-207
Racism   11,34,54-66,73,108-109
Semantic space   12,120-121,130-138
Sexuality   37-39,146-148,174-186
Symbolic interaction   83-84,96-98,167-169,190-192
    labeling wimmin deviant 40-42,69-70,161-164,174-177,186
Wimmin's movement   23,34-35,37-38,48,59,63-65,174,177,
       181,187-188,190,193-194,198-200
Wimmin's Studies   106-107,109,112,187-190,198-200
Work   27-30,55-56,65,120-121,144-145
    academics   2-3,7,13-15,48-53,59,70-71,
        187-190,199-200,212-215
    farm workers   62
    health workers   80-81,120,161
    houseworkers   29-30,144-145,166
    student   5,7-8,82-83
Working class wimmin   165-167,181-182
Victimization   7-9,41-42,48-49,190-191,206-207
    sexual assault   67-81,182-183,204,206-207

Women's Studies

1. Nebraska Sociological Feminist Collective, **A Feminist Ethic for Social Science Research**
2. Mimi Scarf, **Battered Jewish Wives: Case Studies in the Response to Rage**
3. Lynette J. Eastland, **Sociological Organization and Change Within A Feminist Context: A Participant Observation of a Feminist Cooperative**